Great Epochs In American History Vol.-1

by

Francis W. Halsey

Great Epochs In American History Vol.-1

by Francis W. Halsey

ISBN: 978-93-59320-32-8

Published by

DOUBLE 9 BOOKS

2/13-B, Ansari Road
Daryaganj, New Delhi – 110002
info@double9books.com
www.double9books.com
Tel. 011-40042856

This book is under public domain

ABOUT THE AUTHOR

Francis Whiting Halsey (October 15, 1851 - November 24, 1919) was a New York-born American journalist, editor, and historian. He was the son of Civil War Physician Dr. Gaius Leonard Halsey and Juliet (Cartington) Halsey. He was the grandson of Dr. Gaius and Mary (Church) Halsey of Kortright, New York, and a descendant of Thomas Halsey, who arrived from England about 1640 and helped create Southampton, Long Island, one of New York's early English colonies.

CONTENTS

PREFACE

In these ten volumes the aim has been to present striking accounts of ten great epochs in the history of the United States, from the landing of Columbus to the building of the Panama Canal. In large part, events composing each epoch are described by men who participated in them, or were personal eye-witnesses of them.

Columbus, for example, described his own first voyage; Washington, the defeat of Braddock; Gen. "Sam" Houston the battle of San Jacinto; General Robert E. Lee, the capture of John Brown at Harper's Ferry; Murat Halstead, the nomination of Lincoln; Jefferson Davis, the evacuation of Richmond, and his own arrest in Georgia by Federal troops; Mrs. James Chesnut, wife of the Confederate general, the firing on Fort Sumter; Edmund Clarence Stedman, the retreat from Bull Run; Gen. James Longstreet, Pickett's charge at Gettysburg; General Sheridan, Sheridan's ride to Winchester; James G. Blaine, the funeral of Lincoln; Cyrus W. Field, the laying of the Atlantic cable; Horace White, the great Chicago fire; William Jennings Bryan, the first Bryan campaign; Admiral Dewey, the battle of Manila Bay, and Admiral Peary, the finding of the North Pole.

These accounts are often supplemented by passages from the writings of historians and biographers, including George Bancroft, Washington Irving, Francis Parkman, Richard Hildreth, William E.H. Lecky, James Schouler, and John Fiske; or from those of statesmen, journalists and publicists, among them, Thomas Jefferson, John Adams, Thomas H. Benton, Robert Toombs, Horace Greeley, "Bull Run" Russell, Carl Schurz, and Theodore Roosevelt.

The tables of contents prefixt to the several volumes, or the index appended to the last, will show how wide is the range of topics. The events described have been of vital, and often of transcendant, importance to this country and Europe. The writers will be found interesting as authorities, and are often supremely competent, alike as authorities and writers. The work is believed to present American history in a form that will appeal to readers for its authenticity and its novelty.

Francis W. Halsey.

INTRODUCTION

(Voyages of Discovery and Early Explorations.)

Schoolboys have been taught from their earliest years that Columbus discovered America. Few events in prehistoric times seem more probable now than that Columbus was not the first to discover it. The importance of his achievement over that of others lay in his own faith in his success, in his definiteness of purpose, and in the fact that he awakened in Europe an interest in the discovery that led to further explorations, disclosing a new continent and ending in permanent settlements.

The earliest voyages to America, made probably from Asia, led to settlements, but they remained unknown ever afterward to all save the settlers themselves, while those from Europe led to settlements that were either soon abandoned or otherwise came to nought. Wandering Tatar, Chinese, Japanese, Malay, or Polynesian sailors who drifted, intentionally or accidentally, to the Pacific coast in some unrecorded and prehistoric past, and from whom the men we call our aborigines probably are descended, sent back to Asia no tidings of what they had found. Their discovery, in so far as it concerned the people of the Old World, remained as if it had never been.

The hardy Northmen of the Viking age, who, like John Smith, six hundred years afterward, found in Vinland "a pleasant land to see," understood so little of the importance of what they had found, that, by the next century, their discovery had virtually been forgotten in all Scandinavia. It seems never to have become known anywhere else in Europe. Indeed, had the Northmen made it known to other Europeans, it is quite unlikely that any active interest would have been taken in it. Europe in the year 1000 was self-centered. She had troubles enough to absorb all her energies. Ambition for the expansion of her territory, for trade with peoples beyond the great waters, nowhere existed. Most European states were engaged in a grim struggle to hold what they had—to hold it from the aggressions of their neighbors, to hold it against the rising power of Islam.

Columbus did not know he had discovered the continent we call America. He died in the belief that he had found unknown parts of Asia;

that he had discovered a shorter and safer route for trade with the East, and that he had given new proof of the assertions made by astronomers that the earth is round. The men who immediately followed him—Vespucius and the Cabots—believed only that they had confirmed and extended his discovery. Cabot first found the mainland of North America, Vespucius the mainland of South America, but neither knew he had found a new continent. Each saw only coast lines; made landings, it is true; saw and conversed with natives, and Vespucius fought with natives; but of the existence of a new world, having continents comparable to Europe, Asia, or Africa, with an ocean on both sides of them, neither ever so much as dreamed.

Under the splendid inspiration of Prince Henry the Navigator, an inspiration that remained potent throughout Portugal long after his death, Bartholomew Dias, five years before Columbus made his voyage to America, rounded the Cape of Good Hope, actually sailed into the Indian Ocean, and was pressing on toward India when his crew, from exhaustion, refused to go farther, and he was forced to return home. Vasco da Gama, ten years later (1497), following the route of Dias, actually reached India and thus demonstrated that, instead of going overland by caravan, India could be reached by sailing around two-thirds of Africa.

Spanish and Portuguese navigators—Columbus, Da Gama, Dias— alike sought a new and shorter route for trade with the Far East—one, moreover, that would not be molested by the advancing and aggressive Turks. Columbus believed, and so believed Spain and Portugal, that he had found a shorter route than the one Diaz and Da Gama found. Disputes arose between the rival powers as to titles and benefits from the discoveries, and it was because of these that Pope Alexander VI issued his famous Bull, dividing between the two all lands discovered by the navigators, an act which, in our time, has become a curious anomaly, since later proof of the existence of continents between the Atlantic and Pacific made the Pope's decree virtually a partitioning of all America between two favored countries as sole beneficiaries.

Da Gama returned from India laden with Eastern treasure. Columbus returned from America poorer than when he sailed from the port of Palos. Columbus was believed to have found Asia, but he brought home, after several voyages, none of the wealth of Asia. Hence those fierce storms that beat about his head, leading to his imprisonment and to his death in Valladolid, a broken-hearted man.

The Spanish explorers who in the next century followed Columbus, came to America in pursuit of silver and gold. Rich stores had already been found by their countrymen in Mexico and the Peruvian Andes. In meetings with Indians farther north wearing ornaments of gold, the new explorers became convinced that mineral wealth also existed in the lands now called the United States, and especially in the fabled "Seven Cities of Cibola," in the Southwest. Out of this belief came the bold enterprises of Ponce de Leon, De Vaca, Coronado and De Soto, while out of the Spanish successes in finding gold in America came the first known voyage into New York Harbor, that of Verazzano, the Italian in French service, who was seeking Spanish vessels returning richly laden.

Of the French and English explorers of later years—Cartier, Champlain, Marquette, Hudson, Drake—who came to Cape Breton, the St. Lawrence, Hudson, and Mississippi valleys, the California coast—the motives were different. These came to fish for cod, to explore the country, to plant the banners of the Sun King and Queen Bess over new territories, to convert the Indians, to find a northwest passage—that problem of the navigators which baffled them all until 1854—362 years after the landing of Columbus—when an English ship, under Sir Robert McClure, sailed from Bering Sea to Davis Strait, and thus proved that America, North and South, was an island.

Spaniards, however, had dreamed of a northwest passage before any of these. When Magellan passed through the strait that bears his name, and his ship completed the first circumnavigation of the globe, men began first to see that America was no part of Asia. In further proof they sought to find a passage into the Pacific from the north, as a complement to Magellan's passage from the south. Such an attempt was first made by the Spaniards under Vasquez d'Ayllon, four years after the voyage of Magellan; that is, in 1524. Ayllon was hoping to find this passage when he put in at Hampton Roads, just as Hudson hoped to find it, eighty-five years afterward, when he entered the harbor of New York—Hudson, who in a later voyage, sought it once more in Hudson Bay, and perished miserably there, set adrift in an open boat and abandoned by his own mutinous sailors.

F.W.H.

DISCOVERIES BEFORE COLUMBUS

I-THE MEN FROM ASIA AND FROM NORWAY [1]

BY JUSTIN WINSOR

There is not a race of eastern Asia—Siberian, Tatar, Chinese, Japanese, Malay, with the Polynesians—which has not been claimed as discoverers, intending or accidental, of American shores, or as progenitors, more or less perfect or remote, of American peoples; and there is no good reason why any one of them may not have done all that is claimed. The historical evidence, however, is not such as is based on documentary proofs of indisputable character, and the recitals advanced are often far from precise enough to be convincing in details, if their general authenticity is allowed.

Nevertheless, it is much more than barely probable that the ice of Bering Straits or the line of the Aleutian Islands was the pathway of successive immigrations, on occasions perhaps far apart, or maybe near together; and there is hardly a stronger demonstration of such a connection between the two continents than the physical resemblances of the peoples now living on the opposite sides of the Pacific Ocean in these upper latitudes, with the similarity of the flora which environs them on either shore.

It is quite as conceivable that the great northern current, setting east athwart the Pacific, should from time to time have carried along disabled vessels, and stranded them on the shores of California and farther north leading to the infusion of Asiatic blood among whatever there may have been antecedent or autochthonous in the coast peoples. It is certainly in this way possible that the Chinese or Japanese may have helped populate the western slopes of the American continent. There is no improbability even of the Malays of southeastern Asia extending step by step to the Polynesian Islands, and among them and beyond them, till the shores of a new world finally received the impress of their footsteps and of their ethnic characteristics. We may very likely recognize not proofs, but indications, along the shores of South America, that its original people constituted such a stock or were increased by it.

As respects the possible early connections of America on the side of Europe, there is an equally extensive array of claims, and they have been set forth, first and last, with more persistency than effect....

Leaving the old world by the northern passage, Iceland lies at the threshold of America. It is nearer to Greenland than to Norway, and Greenland is but one of the large islands into which the arctic currents divide the North American continent. Thither, to Iceland, if we identify the localities in Geoffrey of Monmouth, King Arthur sailed as early as the beginning of the sixth century, and overcame whatever inhabitants he may have found there. Here, too, an occasional wandering pirate or adventurous Dane had glimpsed the coast. Thither, among others, came the Irish, and in the ninth century we find Irish monks and a small colony of their countrymen in possession. Thither the Gulf Stream carries the southern driftwood, suggesting sunnier lands to whatever race had been allured or driven to its shelter. Here Columbus, when, as he tells us, he visited the island in 1477, found no ice. So that, if we may place reliance on the appreciable change of climate by the precession of the equinoxes, a thousand years ago and more, when the Norwegians crossed from Scandinavia and found these Christian Irish there, the island was not the forbidding spot that it seems with the lapse of centuries to be becoming.

It was in A.D. 875 that Ingolf, a jarl of Norway, came to Iceland with Norse settlers. They built their habitation at first where a pleasant headland seemed attractive, the present Ingolfshofdi, and later founded Reikjavik, where the signs directed them; for certain carved posts, which they had thrown overboard as they approached the island, were found to have drifted to that spot. The Christian Irish preferred to leave their asylum rather than consort with the newcomers, and so the island was left to be occupied by successive immigrations of the Norse, which their king could not prevent. In the end, and within half a century, a hardy little republic—as for a while it was—of near 70,000 inhabitants, was established almost under the arctic circle.

The very next year (A.D. 876) after Ingolf had come to Iceland, a sea-rover, Gunnbiorn, driven in his ship westerly, sighted a strange land, and the report that he made was not forgotten. Fifty years later, more or less, for we must treat the dates of the Icelandic sagas with some reservation, we learn that a wind-tossed vessel was thrown upon a coast far away, which was called Iceland the Great. Then, again, we read of a young Norwegian, Eric the Red, not apparently averse to a brawl, who killed his man in Norway and fled to Iceland, where he kept his dubious character; and again outraging the laws, he was sent into temporary banishment—this time in a ship which he fitted out for discovery; and so he sailed away in the direction of Gunnbiorn's land, and found it. He whiled away three years on its coast, and as soon as he was allowed, ventured back with the tidings. While, to propitiate intending settlers, he said he had been to Greenland, and so the land got a sunny name.

The next year, which seems to have been A.D. 985, he started on his return with 35 ships, but only fourteen of them reached the land. Whenever there was a habitable fiord, a settlement grew up, and the stream of immigrants was for a while constant and considerable. Just at the end of the century (A.D. 999) Lief, a son of Eric, sailed back to Norway, and found the country in the early fervor of a new religion; for King Olaf Tryggvesson had embraced Christianity, and was imposing it on his people. Leif accepted the new faith, and a priest was assigned to him to take back to Greenland; and thus Christianity was introduced into arctic America. So they began to build churches in Greenland, the considerable ruins of one of which stands to this day. The winning of Iceland to the Church was accomplished at the same time....

In the next year after the second voyage of Eric the Red, one of the ships which were sailing from Iceland to the new settlement, was driven far off her course, according to the sagas, and Bjarni Herjulfson, who commanded the vessel, reported that he had come upon a land, away to the southwest, where the coast country was level; and he added that when he turned north it took him nine days to reach Greenland. Fourteen years later than this voyage of Bjarni, which was said to have been in A.D. 986—that is, in the year 1000 or thereabouts—Lief, the same who had brought the Christian priest to Greenland, taking with him 35 companions, sailed from Greenland in quest of the land seen by Bjarni, which Lief first found, where a barren shore stretched back to ice-covered mountains, and, because of the stones there, he called the region Helluland. Proceeding farther south, he found a sandy shore, with a level forest country back of it, and because of the woods it was named Markland. Two days later they came upon other land, and tasting the dew upon the grass they found it sweet. Farther south and westerly they went, and going up a river, came into an expanse of water, where on the shores they built huts to lodge in for the winter, and sent out exploring parties. In one of these Tyrker, a native of a part of Europe where grapes grew, found vines hung with their fruit, which induced Lief to call the country Vinland.

Attempts have been made to identify these various regions by the inexact accounts of the direction of their sailing, by the very general descriptions of the country, by the number of days occupied in going from one point to another, with the uncertainty if the ship sailed at night, and by the length of the shortest day in Vinland—the last a statement that might help us, if it could be interpreted with a reasonable concurrence of opinion, and if it were not confused with other inexplicable statements. The next year Lief's brother, Thorwald, went to Vinland with a single ship, and passed three winters there, making explorations meanwhile, south and north. Thorfinn Karlsefne, arriving in Greenland in A.D. 1006, married a courageous widow named Gudrid, who induced him to sail with his ships to Vinland and make there a permanent settlement, taking with him livestock and other necessaries for colonization. Their first winter in the place was a severe one; but Gudrid gave birth to a son, Snorre, from whom it is claimed Thorwaldsen, the Danish sculptor, was descended. The next season they removed to the spot where Leif had wintered, and called the bay Hop. Having spent a third winter in the country, Karlsefne, with a part of the colony, returned to Greenland.

The saga then goes on to say that trading voyages to the settlement which had been formed by Karlsefne now became frequent, and that the chief lading of the return voyages was timber, which was much needed in Greenland. A bishop of Greenland, Eric Upsi, is also said to have gone to Vinland in A.D. 1121. In 1347 the last ship of which we have any record in these sagas went to Vinland after timber. After this all is oblivion.

There are in all these narratives many details beyond this outline, and those who have sought to identify localities have made the most they could of the mention of a rock here or a bluff there, of an island where they killed a bear, of others where they found eggs, of a headland where they buried a leader who had been killed, of a cape shaped like a keel, of broadfaced natives who offered furs for red cloths, of beaches where they hauled up their ships, and of tides that were strong; but the more these details are scanned in the different sagas, the more they confuse the investigator, and the more successive relators try to enlighten us the more our doubts are strengthened, till we end with the conviction that all attempts at consistent unravelment leave nothing but a vague sense of something somewhere done.

II-HOW THE NORWEGIANS CAME TO VINLAND [1]

(1000 A.D.)

Lief invited his father, Eric, to become the leader of the expedition, but Eric declined, saying that he was then stricken in years, and adding that he was less able to endure the exposure of sea life than he had been. Lief replied that he would, nevertheless, be the one who would be most apt to bring good luck, and Eric yielded to Lief's solicitation, and rode from home when they were ready to sail.

They put the ship in order; and, when they were ready, they sailed out to sea, and found first that land which Bjarni and his shipmates found last. They sailed up to the land and cast anchor, and launched a boat and went ashore, and saw no grass there. Great ice mountains lay inland back from the sea, and it was as a [table-land of] flat rock all the way from the sea to the ice mountains; and the country seemed to them to be entirely devoid of good qualities. Then said Lief, "It has not come to pass with us in regard to this land as with Biarni, that we have not gone upon it. To this country I will now give a name, and call it Helluland," They returned to the ship, put out to sea, and found a second land.

They sailed again to the land, and came to anchor, and launched the boat, and went ashore. This was a level wooded land; and there were broad stretches of white sand where they went, and the land was level by the sea. Then said Lief, "This land shall have a name after its nature; and we will call it Markland." They returned to the ship forthwith, and sailed away upon the main with northeast winds, and were out two "doegr" before they sighted land. They sailed toward this land, and came to an island which lay to the northward off the land. There they went ashore and looked about them, the weather being fine, and they observed that there was dew upon the grass, and it so happened that they touched the dew with their hands, and touched their hands to their mouths, and it seemed to them that they had never before tasted anything so sweet as this....

A cargo sufficient for the ship was cut, and when the spring came they made their ship ready, and sailed away; and from its products Lief gave the land a name, and called it Wineland. They sailed out to sea, and had fair winds until they sighted Greenland and the fells below the glaciers. Then one of the men spoke up and said, "Why do you steer the ship so much into the wind?" Lief answers: "I have my mind upon my steering, but on other matters as well. Do ye not see anything out of the common?" They replied that they saw nothing strange. "I do not know," says Lief, "whether it is a ship or a skerry that I see." Now they saw it, and said that it must be a skerry; but he was so much keener of sight than they that he was able to discern men upon the skerry. "I think it best to tack," says Lief, "so that we may draw near to them, that we may be able to render them assistance if they should stand in need of it; and, if they should not be peaceable disposed, we shall still have better command of the situation than they."

They approached the skerry, and, lowering their sail, cast anchor, and launched a second small boat, which they had brought with them. Tyrker inquired who was the leader of the party. He replied that his name was Thori, and that he was a Norseman; "but what is thy name?" Lief gave his name. "Art thou a son of Eric the Red of Brattahlid?" says he. Lief responded that he was. "It is now my wish," says Lief, "to take you all into my ship, and likewise so much of your possessions as the ship will hold." This offer was accepted, and [with their ship] thus laden they held away to Ericsfirth, and sailed until they arrived at Brattahlid. Having discharged the cargo, Lief invited Thori, with his wife, Gudrid, and three others, to make their home with him, and procured quarters for the other members of the crew, both for his own and Thori's men. Lief rescued fifteen persons from the skerry. He was afterward called Lief the Lucky. Lief had now a goodly store both of property and honor. There was serious illness that winter in Thori's party, and Thori and a great number of his people died. Eric the Red also died that winter. There was now much talk about Lief's Wineland journey; and his brother, Thorvald, held that the country had not been sufficiently explored. Thereupon Lief said to Thorvald, "If it be thy will, brother, thou mayest go to Wineland with my ship; but I wish the ship first to fetch the wood which Thori had upon the skerry." And so it was done.

Now Thorvald, with the advice of his brother, Lief, prepared to make this voyage with thirty men. They put their ship in order, and sailed out to sea; and there is no account of their voyage before their arrival at Liefs-booths in Wineland. They laid up their ship there, and remained there quietly during the winter, supplying themselves with food by fishing. In the spring, however, Thorvald said that they should put their ship in order, and that a few men should take the after-boat, and proceed along the western coast, and explore [the region] thereabouts during the summer. They found it a fair, well-wooded country. It was but a short distance from the woods to the sea, and [there were] white sands, as well as great numbers of islands and shallows. They found neither dwelling of man nor lair of beast; but in one of the westerly islands they found a wooden building for the shelter of grain. They found no other trace of human handiwork; and they turned back, and arrived at Liefs-booths in the autumn.

The following summer Thorvald set out toward the east with the ship, and along the northern coast. They were met by a high wind off a certain promontory, and were driven ashore there, and damaged the keel of their ship, and were compelled to remain there for a long time and repair the injury to their vessel. Then said Thorvald to his companions, "I propose that we raise the keel upon this cape, and call it Keelness"; and so they did. Then they sailed away to the eastward off the land and into the mouth of the adjoining firth and to a headland, which projected into the sea there, and which was entirely covered with woods. They found an anchorage for their ship, and put out the gangway to the land; and Thorvald and all of his companions went ashore. "It is a fair region here," said he; "and here I should like to make my home."

They then returned to the ship, and discovered on the sands, in beyond the headland, three mounds: they went up to these, and saw that they were three skin canoes with three men under each. They thereupon divided their party, and succeeded in seizing all the men but one, who escaped with his canoe. They killed the eight men, and then ascended the headland again, and looked about them, and discovered within the firth certain hillocks, which they concluded must be habitations. They were then so overpowered with sleep that they could not keep awake, and all fell into a [heavy] slumber from which they were awakened by the sound of a cry uttered above them; and the words of the cry were these: "Awake, Thorvald, thou and all thy company, if thou wouldst save thy life; and board thy ship with all thy men, and sail with all speed from the land!" A countless number of skin canoes then advanced toward them from the inner part of the firth, whereupon Thorvald ex-claimed, "We must put out the war-boards on both sides of the ship, and defend ourselves to the best of our ability, but offer little attack." This they did; and the Skrellings, after they had shot at them for a time, fled precipitately, each as best he could. Thorvald then inquired of his men whether any of them had been wounded, and they informed him that no one of them had received a wound. "I have been wounded in my arm-pit," says he. "An arrow flew in between the gunwale and the shield, below my arm. Here is the shaft, and it will bring me to my end. I counsel you now to retrace your way with the utmost speed. But me ye shall convey to that headland which seemed to me to offer so pleasant a dwelling-place: thus it may be fulfilled that the truth sprang to my lips when I exprest the wish to abide there for a time. Ye shall bury me there, and place a cross at my head, and another at my feet, and call it Crossness forever after." At that time Christianity had obtained in Greenland: Eric the Red died, however, before [the introduction of] Christianity.

Thorvald died; and, when they had carried out his injunctions, they took their departure, and rejoined their companions, and they told each other of the experiences which had befallen them. They remained there during the winter, and gathered grapes and wood with which to freight the ship. In the following spring they returned to Greenland, and arrived with their ship in Ericsfirth, where they were able to recount great tidings to Lief....

There was now much talk anew about a Wineland voyage, for this was reckoned both a profitable and an honorable enterprise. The same summer that Karlsefni arrived from Wineland a ship from Norway arrived in Greenland. This ship was commanded by two brothers, Helgi and Finnbogi, who passed the winter in Greenland. They were descended from an Icelandic family of the East-firths. It is now to be added that Freydis, Eric's daughter, set out from her home at Gardar, and waited upon the brothers, Helgi and Finnbogi, and invited them to sail with their vessel to Wineland, and to share with her equally all of the good things which they might succeed in obtaining there. To this they agreed, and she departed thence to visit her brother Lief, and ask him to give her the house which he had caused to be erected in Wineland; but he made her the same answer [as that which he had given Karlsefni], saying that he would lend the house, but not give it. It was stipulated between Karlsefni and Freydis that each should have on shipboard thirty able-bodied men, besides the women; but Freydis immediately violated this compact by concealing five men more [than this number], and this the brothers did not discover before they arrived in Wineland. They now put out to sea, having agreed beforehand that they would sail in company, if possible, and, altho they were not far apart from each other, the brothers arrived somewhat in advance, and carried their belongings up to Lief's house.

III-THE FIRST CHILD OF EUROPEAN
RACE BORN IN AMERICA [1]

(About 1000 A.D.)

One summer a ship came from Norway to Greenland. The skipper's name was Thorfinn Karlsefni, and he was the son of Thord, called "Horsehead," and a grandson of Snorri. Thorfinn Karlsefni, who was a very wealthy man, passed the winter there in Greenland, with Lief Ericsson. He very soon set his heart upon a maiden called Gudrid, and sought her hand in marriage.

That same winter a new discussion arose concerning a Wineland voyage. The people urged Rarlsefni to make the bold venture, so he determined to undertake the voyage, and gathered a company of sixty men and five women. He entered into an agreement with his shipmates that they should each share equally in all the spoils. They took with them all kinds of cattle, as they intended to settle the country if they could. Karlsefni asked Lief for his house in Wineland. Lief replied that he would lend it but not give it.

They sailed out to sea with the ship, and arrived safe and sound at Lief's booths, and carried their hammocks ashore there. They were soon provided with an abundant supply of food, for a whale of good size and quality was driven ashore, and they secured it. Their cattle were turned out upon the land. Karlsefni ordered trees to be felled; for he needed timber wherewith to load his ships. They gathered some of all the products of the land—grapes, all kinds of game, fish, and other good things.

In the summer after the first winter the Skrellings [2] were discovered. A great throng of men came forth from the woods; the cattle were close by and the bull began to bellow and roar with a great noise. At this the Skrellings were frightened and ran away with their packs, wherein were gray furs, sables, and all kinds of skins. They fled toward Karlsefni's dwelling and tried to get into the house, but Karlsefni caused the doors to be defended. Neither people could understand the other's language. The Skrellings put down their packs, then opened them and offered their wares in exchange for weapons, but Karlsefni forbade his men to sell their weapons. He bade the women to carry out milk to the Skrellings; as soon as these people had tasted the milk, they wanted to buy it and nothing else.

Now it is to be told that Karlsefni caused a strong wooden palisade to be constructed and set up around the house. It was at this time that a baby boy was born to Gudrid and Karlsefni, and he was called Snorri. In the early part of the second winter the Skrellings came to them again in greater numbers than before, and brought with them the same kind of wares to exchange. Then said Karlsefni to the women, "Do ye carry out now the same thing which proved so profitable before, and nothing else." The Skrellings seemed contented at first, but soon after, while Gudrid was sitting in the doorway beside the cradle of her infant son, Snorri, she heard a great crash made by one of the Skrellings who had tried to seize a man's weapons. One of Karlsefni's followers killed him for it. "Now we must needs take counsel together," said Karlsefni, "for I believe they will visit us a third time in greater numbers. Let us now adopt this plan: when the tribe approaches from the forest, ten of our number shall go out upon the cape in front of our houses and show themselves there, while the remainder of our company shall go into the woods back of our houses and hew a clearing for our cattle. Then we will take our bull and let him go in advance of us to meet the enemy." The next time the Skrellings came they found Karlsefni's men ready and fled helter-skelter into the woods. Karlsefni and his party remained there throughout the winter, but in the spring Karlsefni announced that he did not intend to remain there longer, for he wished to return with his wife and son to Greenland. They now made ready for the voyage and carried away with them much in vines and grapes and skins.

IV-OTHER PRE-COLUMBIAN VOYAGES [1]

BY HENRY WHEATON

No subsequent traces of the Norman colony in America are to be found until the year 1059, when it is said that an Irish or Saxon priest, named Jon or John, who had preached for some time as a missionary in Iceland, went to Vinland, for the purpose of converting the colonists to Christianity, where he was murdered by the heathens. A bishop of Greenland, named Erik, afterward (A.D. 1121) undertook the same voyage, for the same purpose, but with what success is uncertain. The authenticity of the Icelandic accounts of the discovery and settlement of Vinland were recognized in Denmark shortly after this period by King Svend Estrithson, or Sweno II, in a conversation which Adam of Bremen had with this monarch. But no further mention is made of them in the national annals, and it may appear doubtful what degree of credit is due to the relations of the Venetian navigators, the two brothers Zeni, who are said to have sailed in the latter part of the fourteenth century, in the service of a Norman prince of the Orcades, to the coasts of New England, Carolina, and even Mexico, or at least to have collected authentic accounts of voyages as far west and south as these countries. The land diseovered and peopled by the Norwegians is called by Antonio Zeni, Estotoland, and he states, among other particulars, that the princes of the country still had in their possession Latin books, which they did not understand, and which were probably those left by the bishop Erik during his mission.

Supposing these latter discoveries to be authentic, they could hardly have escaped the attention of Columbus, who had himself navigated in the arctic seas, but whose mind dwelt with such intense fondness upon his favorite idea of finding a passage to the East Indies, across the western ocean, that he might have neglected these indications of the existence of another continent in the direction pursued by the Venetian adventurers.

At all events, there is not the silghtest reason to believe that the illustrious Genoese was acquainted with the discovery of North America by the Normans five centuries before his time, however well authenticated that fact now appears to be by the Icelandic records to which we have referred. The colony established by them probably perished in the same manner with the ancient establishments in Greenland. Some faint traces of its existence may, perhaps, be found in the relations of the Jesuit missionaries respecting a native tribe in the district of Gaspe, at the mouth of the St. Lawrence, who are said to have attained a certain degree of civilization, to have worshiped the sun, and observed the position of the stars. Others revered the symbol of the cross before the arrival of the French missionaries, which, according to their tradition, had been taught them by a venerable person who cured, by this means, a terrible epidemic which raged among them.

THE DISCOVERY BY COLUMBUS (1492)

I-AS DESCRIBED BY WASHINGTON IRVING [1]

It was early in the morning of Friday, the 3d of August, 1492, that Columbus set sail from the bar of Saltes, a small island formed by the rivers Odiel and Tinto, in front of Palos, steering for the Canary Islands, from whence he intended to strike due west. As a guide by which to sail, he had the conjectural map or chart sent him by Paolo Toscanelli, of Florence. In this it is supposed the coasts of Europe and Africa, from the south of Ireland to the end of Guinea, were delineated as immediately opposite to the extremity of Asia, while the great island of Cipango, described by Marco Polo, lay between them, 1,500 miles from the Asiatic coast. At this island Columbus expected first to arrive....

On losing sight of this last trace of land, the hearts of the crews failed them, for they seemed to have taken leave of the world. Behind them was everything dear to the heart of man—country, family, friends, life itself; before them everything was chaos, mystery, and peril. In the perturbation of the moment they despaired of ever more seeing their homes. Many of the rugged seamen shed tears, and some broke into loud lamentations. Columbus tried in every way to soothe their distress, describing the splendid countries to which he expected to conduct them, promising them land, riches, and everything that could arouse their cupidity or inflame their imaginations; nor were these promises made for purposes of deception, for he certainly believed he should realize them all.

He now gave orders to the commanders of the other vessels, in case they should be separated by any accident, to continue directly westward; but that, after sailing 700 leagues, they should lay by from midnight until daylight, as at about that distance he confidently expected to find land. Foreseeing that the vague terrors already awakened among the seamen would increase with the space which intervened between them and their homes, he commenced a stratagem which he continued throughout the voyage. This was to keep two reckonings, one private, in which the true way of the ship was noted, and which he retained in secret for his own government; the other public, for general inspection, in which a number of leagues was daily subtracted from the sailing of the ships so as to keep the crews in ignorance of the real distance they had advanced....

On the 13th of September, in the evening, Columbus, for the first time, noticed the variation of the needle, a phenomenon which had never before been remarked. He at first made no mention of it, lest his people should be alarmed; but it soon attracted the attention of the pilots, and filled them with consternation. It seemed as if the very laws of nature were changing as they advanced, and that they were entering another world, subject to unknown influences. They apprehended that the compass was about to lose its mysterious virtues, and, without this guide, what was to become of them in a vast and trackless ocean? Columbus tasked his science and ingenuity for reasons with which to allay their terrors. He told them that the direction of the needle was not to the polar star, but to some fixt and invisible point. The variation, therefore, was not caused by any fallacy in the compass, but by the movement of the north star itself, which, like the other heavenly bodies, had its changes and revolutions, and every day described a circle round the pole. The high opinion they entertained of Columbus as a profound astronomer gave weight to his theory, and their alarm subsided.

They had now arrived within the influence of the trade-wind, which, following the sun, blows steadily from east to west between the tropics, and sweeps over a few adjoining degrees of the ocean. With this propitious breeze directly aft, they were wafted gently but speedily over a tranquil sea, so that for many days they did not shift a sail. Columbus in his journal perpetually recurs to the bland and temperate serenity of the weather, and compares the pure and balmy mornings to those of April in Andalusia, observing that the song of the nightingale was alone wanting to complete the illusion....

They now began to see large patches of herbs and weeds, all drifting from the west. Some were such as grow about rocks or in rivers, and as green as if recently washed from the land. On one of the patches was a live crab. They saw also a white tropical bird, of a kind which never sleeps upon the sea; and tunny-fish played about the ships. Columbus now supposed himself arrived in the weedy sea described by Aristotle, into which certain ships of Cadiz had been driven by an impetuous east wind.

As he advanced, there were various other signs that gave great animation to the crews; many birds were seen flying from the west; there was a cloudiness in the north, such as often hangs over land; and at sunset the imagination of the seamen, aided by their desires, would shape those clouds into distant islands. Every one was eager to be the first to behold and announce the wished-for shore; for the sovereigns had promised a pension of thirty crowns to whomsoever should first discover land. Columbus sounded occasionally with a line of 200 fathoms, but found no bottom. Martin Alonzo Pinzon, as well as others of his officers and many of the seamen, were often solicitous for Columbus to alter his course and steer in the direction of these favorable signs; but he persevered in steering to the westward, trusting that by keeping in one steady direction, he should reach the coast of India, even if he should miss the intervening islands, and might then seek them on his return....

The situation of Columbus was daily becoming more and more critical. The impatience of the seamen arose to absolute mutiny. They gathered together in the retired parts of the ships, at first in little knots of two and three, which gradually increased and became formidable, joining in murmurs and menaces against the admiral. They exclaimed against him as an ambitious desperado who, in a mad fantasy, had determined to do something extravagant to render himself notorious. What obligation bound them to persist, or when were the terms of their agreement to be considered as fulfilled? They had already penetrated into seas untraversed by a sail, and where man had never before adventured. Were they to sail on until they perished, or until all return with their frail ships became impossible? Who would blame them should they consult their safety and return? The admiral was a foreigner, a man without friends or influence. His scheme had been condemned by the learned as idle and visionary, and discountenanced by people of all ranks. There was, therefore, no party on his side, but rather a large number who would be gratified by his failure.

Such are some of the reasonings by which these men prepared themselves for open rebellion. Some even proposed, as an effectual mode of silencing all after complaints of the admiral, that they should throw him into the sea, and give out that he had fallen overboard while contemplating the stars and signs of the heavens, with his astronomical instruments.

Columbus was not ignorant of these secret cabals, but he kept a serene and steady countenance, soothing some with gentle words, stimulating the pride or the avarice of others, and openly menacing the most refractory with punishment. New hopes diverted them for a time. On the 25th of September Martin Pinzon mounted on the stern of his vessel and shouted, "Land! land! Senor, I claim the reward!" There was, indeed, such an appearance of land in the southwest that Columbus threw himself upon his knees and returned thanks to God, and all the crews joined in chanting Gloria in Excelsis. The ships altered their course and stood all night to the southwest, but the morning light put an end to all their hopes as to a dream; the fancied land proved to be nothing but an evening cloud, and had vanished in the night....

He was now at open defiance with his crew, and his situation would have been desperate, but, fortunately, the manifestations of land on the following day were such as no longer to admit of doubt. A green fish, such as keeps about rocks, swam by the ships; and a branch of thorn, with berries on it, floated by; they picked up, also, a reed, a small board, and, above all, a staff artificially carved. All gloom and murmuring was now at an end, and throughout the day each one was on the watch for the long-sought land. They continued on their course until two in the morning, when a gun from the Pinto gave the joyful signal of land. It was first discovered by a mariner named Rodriguez Bermejo, resident of Triana, a suburb of Seville, but native of Alcala de la Guadaira; but the reward was afterward adjudged to the admiral, for having previously perceived the light. The land was now clearly seen about two leagues distant, whereupon they took in sail, and laid to, waiting impatiently for the dawn. .

When the day dawned, Columbus saw before him a level and beautiful island, several leagues in extent, of great freshness and verdure, and covered with trees like a continual orchard. Tho everything appeared in the wild luxuriance of untamed nature, yet the island was evidently populous, for the inhabitants were seen issuing from the woods, and running from all parts to the shore. They were all perfectly naked, and, from their attitudes and gestures, appeared lost in astonishment at the sight of the ships. Columbus made signal to cast anchor, and to man the boats. He entered his own boat richly attired in scarlet, and bearing the royal standard. Martin Alonzo Pinzon, and Vicente Yanez, the brother, likewise put off in their boats, each bearing the banner of the enterprise, emblazoned with a green cross, having on each side the letters F and Y, surmounted by crowns, the Spanish initials of the Castilian monarchs, Fernando and Ysabel.

As they approached the shores they were delighted by the beauty and grandeur of the forests; the variety of unknown fruits on the trees which overhung the shores; the purity and suavity of the atmosphere, and the crystal transparency of the seas which bathe these islands. On landing, Columbus threw himself upon his knees, kissed the earth, and returned thanks to God with tears of joy. His example was followed by his companions, whose breasts, indeed, were full to overflowing. Columbus, then rising, drew his sword, displayed the royal standard, and took possession, in the names of the Castilian sovereigns, giving the island the name of San Salvador. He then called upon all present to take the oath of obedience to him, as admiral and viceroy, and representative of the sovereigns.

His followers now burst forth into the most extravagant transports. They thronged around him, some embracing him, others kissing his hands. Those who had been most mutinous and turbulent during the voyage were now most devoted and enthusiastic. Some begged favors of him, as of a man who had already wealth and honors in his gift. Many abject spirits, who had outraged him by their insolence, now crouched at his feet, begging his forgiveness, and offering, for the future, the blindest obedience to his commands.

II-AS DESCRIBED BY COLUMBUS HIMSELF [1]

As I know that it will afford you pleasure that I have brought my undertaking to a successful result, I have determined to write to you this letter to inform you of everything that has been done and discovered in this voyage of mine....

On the thirty-third day after leaving Cadiz I came into the Indian Sea, where I discovered many islands inhabited by numerous people. I took possession of all of them for our most fortunate King by making public proclamation and unfurling his standard, no one making any resistance. To the first of them I have given the name of our blest Savior, trusting in whose aid I had reached this and all the rest; but the Indians call it Guanahani [2] . To each of the others also I gave a new name, ordering one to be called Sancta Maria de Concepcion, another Fernandina, another Hysabella, another Johana; and so with all the rest.

As soon as we reached the island which I have just said was called Johana, I sailed along its coast some considerable distance toward the west, and found it to be so large, without any apparent end, that I believed it was not an island, but a continent, a province of Cathay. But I saw neither towns nor cities lying on the seaboard, only some villages and country farms with whose inhabitants I could not get speech, because they fled as soon as they beheld us. I continued on, supposing I should come to city or country houses. At last, finding that no further discoveries rewarded our progress, and that this course was leading us toward the north, which I was desirous of avoiding, as it was now winter in these regions, and it had always been my intention to proceed southward, and the winds also were favorable to such desires, I concluded not to attempt any other adventures, so, turning back, I came again to a certain harbor, which I had remarked. From there I sent two of our men into the country to learn whether there was any king or cities in that land. They journeyed for three days, and found innumerable people and habitations, but small and having no fixt government, on which account they returned. Meanwhile I had learned from some Indians whom I had seized at this place, that this country was really an island. Consequently, I continued along toward the east, as much as 322 miles, always hugging the shore, where was the very extremity of the island. From there I saw another island to the eastwards, distant 54 miles from this Johana, which I named

Hispana, and proceeded to it, and directed my course for 564 miles east by north as it were, just as I had done at Johana.

The island called Johana, as well as the others in its neighborhood, is exceedingly fertile. It has numerous harbors on all sides, very safe and wide, above comparison with any I have ever seen. Through it flow many very broad and health-giving rivers; and there are in it numerous very lofty mountains. All these islands are very beautiful, and of quite different shapes, easy to be traversed, and full of the greatest variety of trees reaching to the stars. I think these never lose their leaves, as I saw them looking as green and lovely as they are wont to be in the month of May in Spain. Some of them were in leaf, and some in fruit; each flourishing in the condition its nature required. The nightingale was singing and various other little birds, when I was rambling among them in the month of November. There are also in the island called Johana seven or eight kinds of palms, which as readily surpass ours in height and beauty as do all the other trees, herbs, and fruits. There are also wonderful pine-woods, fields, and extensive meadows, birds of various kinds, and honey, and all the different metals except iron.

In the island, which I have said before was called Hispana, there are very lofty and beautiful mountains, great farms, groves and fields, most fertile both for cultivation and for pasturage, and well adapted for constructing buildings. The convenience of the harbors in this island, and the excellence of the rivers, in volume and salubrity, surpass human belief, unless one should see them. In it the trees, pasture-lands, and fruits differ much from those of Johana. Besides, this Hispana abounds in various kinds of spices, gold, and metals.

The inhabitants of both sexes of this and of all the other islands I have seen, or of which I have any knowledge, always go as naked as they came into the world, except that some of the women cover parts of their bodies with leaves or branches, or a veil of cotton, which they prepare themselves for this purpose. They are all, as I said before, unprovided with any sort of iron, and they are destitute of arms, which are entirely unknown to them, and for which they are not adapted; not on account of any bodily deformity, for they are well made, but because they are timid and full of terror. They carry, however, canes dried in the sun in place of weapons, upon whose roots they fix a wooden shaft, dried and sharpened to a point. But they never dare to make use of these, for it has often happened, when I have sent two or three of my men to some of their villages to speak with the inhabitants, that a crowd of Indians has sallied forth; but, when they saw our men approaching, they speedily took to flight, parents abandoning their children, and children their parents.

This happened not because any loss or injury had been inflicted upon any of them. On the contrary, I gave whatever I had, cloth and many other things, to whomsoever I approached, or with whom I could get speech, without any return being made to me; but they are by nature fearful and timid. But, when they see that they are safe, and all fear is banished, they are very guileless and honest, and very liberal of all they have. No one refuses the asker anything that he possesses; on the contrary, they themselves invite us to ask for it. They manifest the greatest affection toward all of us, exchanging valuable things for trifles, content with the very least thing or nothing at all. But I forbade giving them a very trifling thing and of no value, such as bits of plates, dishes, or glass, also nails and straps; altho it seemed to them, if they could get such, that they had acquired the most beautiful jewels in the world.

For it chanced that a sailor received for a single strap as much weight of gold as three gold solidi; and so others for other things of less price, especially for new blancas, and for some gold coins, for which they gave whatever the seller asked; for instance, an ounce and a half or two ounces of gold, or thirty or forty pounds of cotton, with which they were already familiar. So, too, for pieces of hoops, jugs, jars, and pots they bartered cotton and gold like beasts. This I forbade, because it was plainly unjust; and I gave them many beautiful and pleasing things, which I had brought with me, for no return whatever, in order to win their affection, and that they might become Christians and inclined to love our king and queen and princes and all the people of Spain, and that they might be eager to search for and gather and give to us what they abound in and we greatly need.

They do not practise idolatry; on the contrary, they believe that all strength, all power, in short, all blessings, are from heaven, and that I have come down from there with these ships and sailors; and in this spirit was I received everywhere, after they had got over their fear They are neither lazy nor awkward, but, on the contrary, are of an excellent and acute understanding. Those who have sailed these seas give excellent accounts of everything; but they have never seen men wearing clothes, or ships like ours....

As soon as I had come into this sea, I took by force some Indians from the first island, in order that they might learn from us, and at the same time tell us what they knew about affairs in these regions. This succeeded admirably; for in a short time we understood them and they us, both by gesture and signs and words, and they were of great service to us. They are coming now with me, and have always believed that I have come from heaven, notwithstanding the long time they have been, and still remain, with us. They were the first who told this wherever we went, one calling to another, with a loud voice, "Come, come, you will see men from heaven." Whereupon both women and men, children and adults, young and old, laying aside the fear they had felt a little before, flocked eagerly to see us, a great crowd thronging about our steps, some bringing food, and others drink, with greatest love and incredible good will....

I have told already how I sailed in a straight course along the island of Johana from west to east 322 miles. From this voyage and the extent of my journeyings I can say that this Johana is larger than England and Scotland together. For beyond the aforesaid 322 miles, in that portion which looks toward the west, there are two more provinces, which I did not visit. One of them the Indians called Anan, and its inhabitants are born with tails. These provinces extend 180 miles, as I learned from the Indians, whom I am bringing with me, and who are well acquainted with all these islands....

Altho these matters are very wonderful and unheard of, they would have been much more so if the ships to a reasonable amount had been furnished me. But what has been accomplished is great and wonderful, and not at all proportionate to my deserts, but to the sacred Christian faith, and to the piety and religion of our sovereigns. For what the mind of man could not compass, the spirit of God has granted to mortals. For God is wont to listen to his servants who love his precepts, even in impossibilities, as has happened to me in the present instance, who have accomplished what human strength has hitherto never attained. For, if any one has written or told anything about these islands, all have done so either obscurely or by guesswork, so that it has almost seemed to be fabulous.

Therefore let king and queen and princes, and their most fortunate realms, and all other Christian provinces, let us all return thanks to our Lord and Savior Jesus Christ, who has bestowed so great a victory and reward upon us; let there be processions and solemn sacrifices prepared; let the churches be decked with festal boughs; let Christ rejoice upon earth as he rejoices in heaven, as He foresees that so many souls of so many people heretofore lost are to be saved; and let us be glad not only for the exaltation of our faith, but also for the increase of temporal prosperity, in which not only Spain, but all Christendom is about to share.

As these things have been accomplished, so have they been briefly narrated. Farewell.

THE BULL OF POPE ALEXANDER VI. PARTITIONING AMERICA (1493) [1]

The copy of the bull, or donation, by the authority whereof Pope Alexander, the sixth of that name, gave and granted to the kings of Castile and their successors the regions and lands found in the west ocean sea by the navigations of the Spanish.

Alexander, bishop, the servant of the servants of God: To our most dearly beloved son in Christ, King Ferdinand, and to our dearly beloved daughter in Christ, Elizabeth, Queen of Castile, Leon, Aragon, Sicily, and Granada, most noble princes, greeting and apostolic benediction.

Among other works acceptable to the divine majesty and according to our hearts' desire, this certainly is the chief, that the Catholic faith and Christian religion, especially in this our time, may in all places be exalted, amplified, and enlarged, whereby the health of souls may be procured and the barbarous nations subdued and brought to the faith. And therefore, whereas by the favor of God's clemency (altho not without equal deserts), we are called to this holy seat of Peter, and understanding you to be true Catholic Princes as we have ever known you, and as your noble and worthy acts have declared in manner to the whole world, in that, with all your study, diligence, and industry, you have spared no travels, charges or perils, adventuring even the shedding of your own blood, with applying your whole minds and endeavors hereunto, as your noble expeditions achieved in recovering the kingdom of Granada from the tyranny of the Saracens in these our days, do plainly declare your acts with so great glory of the divine name. For the which, as we think you worthy, so ought we of our own free will favorably to grant you all things whereby you may daily, with more fervent minds to the honor of God and enlarging the Christian empire, prosecute your devout and laudable purpose most acceptable to the immortal God.

We are credibly informed that, whereas of late you were determined to seek and find certain islands and firm lands far remote and unknown (and not heretofore found by any other), to the intent to bring the inhabitants of the same to honor our Redeemer and to profess the Catholic faith, you have hitherto been much occupied in the expugnation and recovery of the kingdom of Granada, by reason whereof you could not bring your said laudable purpose to the end desired. Nevertheless, as it hath pleased Almighty God, the aforesaid kingdom being recovered, willing to accomplish your said desire, you have, not without great labor, perils, and charges, appointed our well-beloved son Christopher Columbus (a man very well commended as most worthy and apt for so great a matter), well furnished with men and ships and other necessaries, to seek (by the sea where hitherto no man bath sailed), such firm lands and islands far remote and hitherto unknown.

Who (by God's help), making diligent search in the ocean sea, have found certain remote islands and firm lands which were not heretofore found by any other. In the which (as is said), many nations inhabit, living peacefully and going naked, not accustomed to eat flesh. And as far as your messengers can conjecture, the nations inhabiting the aforesaid lands and islands believe that there is one God creature in heaven: and seem apt to be brought to the embracing of the Catholic faith and to be imbued with good manners: by reason whereof, we may hope that, if they be well instructed, they may easily be induced to receive the name of our Saviour Jesus Christ. We are further advertised that the aforenamed Christopher hath now builded and erected a fortress with good ammunition in one of the aforesaid principal islands, in the which he hath placed a garrison of certain of the Christian men that went thither with him: as well to the intent to defend the same, as also to search other islands and firm lands far remote and yet unknown. We also understand, that in these lands and islands lately found, is great plenty of gold and spices, with divers and many other precious things of sundry kinds and qualities.

Therefore all things diligently considered (especially the amplifying and enlarging of the Catholic faith, as it behooveth Catholic Princes following the examples of your noble progenitors of famous memory), whereas you are determined by the favor of Almighty God, to subdue and bring to the Catholic faith the inhabitants of the aforesaid lands and islands, we greatly commending this, your godly and laudable purpose in our Lord, and desirous to have the same brought to a due end, and the name of our Saviour to be known in those parts, do exhort you in our Lord and by the receiving of your holy baptism whereby you are bound to the Apostolic obedience, and earnestly require you by the bowels of mercy of our Lord Jesus Christ, that, when you intend for the zeal of the Catholic faith to prosecute the said expedition to reduce the people of the aforesaid lands and islands to the Christian religion, you shall spare no labors at any time, or be deterred with any perils conceiving from hope and confidence that the omnipotent God will give good success to your godly attempts.

And that being authorized by the privilege of the Apostolic grace, you may the more freely and boldly take upon you the enterprise of so great a matter, we of our own motion, and not either at your request nor at the instant petition of any other person, but of our own mere liberality and certain science, and by the fulness of Apostolic power, do give, grant, and assign to you, your heirs and successors, all the firm lands and islands found or to be found, discovered or to be discovered toward the west and south, drawing a line from the pole Arctic to the pole Antarctic (that is) from the north to the south: containing in this donation, whatsoever firm lands or islands are found or to be found toward India or toward any other part whatsoever it be, being distant from, or without the aforesaid line drawn a hundred leagues toward the west and south from any of the islands which are commonly called De Los Azores and Cabo Verde. All the islands, therefore, and firm lands, found and to be found, discovered and to be discovered, from the said line toward the west and south, such as have not actually been heretofore possest by any other Christian king or prince until the day of the nativity of our Lord Jesus Christ last passed, from the which beginneth this present year.

We, by the authority of almighty God granted unto us in Saint Peter, and by the office which we bear on the earth in the stead of Jesus Christ, do forever, by the tenure of these presents, give, grant, assign, unto you, your heirs, and successors (the kings of Castile and Leon), all those lands and islands, with their dominions, territories, cities, castles, towers, places, and villages, with all the right and jurisdictions thereunto pertaining: constituting, assigning, and deputing, you, your heirs, and successors the lords thereof, with full and free power, authority, and jurisdiction. Decreeing nevertheless by this, our donation, grant, and assignation, that from no Christian Prince which actually hath possest the aforesaid islands and firm lands unto the day of the nativity of our Lord beforesaid, their right obtained to be understood hereby to be taken away, or that it ought to be taken away.

Furthermore, we command you in the virtue of holy obedience (as you have promised, and we doubt not you will do upon mere devotion and princely magnanimity), to send to the said firm lands and islands honest, virtuous, and learned men, such as fear God, and are able to instruct the inhabitants in the Catholic faith and good manners, applying all their possible diligence in the premises.

We furthermore straightly inhibit all manner of persons, of what state, degree, order, or condition, soever they be, altho of Imperial and regal dignity, under the pain of the sentence of excommunication which they shall incur if they do to the contrary, that they in no case presume special license of you, your heirs, and successors, to travel for merchandise or for any other cause, to the said lands or islands, found or to be found, discovered or to be discovered, toward the west and south, drawing a line from the pole Arctic to the pole Antarctic, whether the firm lands and islands found and to be found, be situated toward India or toward any other part being distant from the line drawn a hundred leagues toward the west from any of the islands commonly called De Los Azores and Cabo Verde: Notwithstanding constitutions, decrees, and apostolic ordinances, whatsoever they are to the contrary:

In him from whom empires, dominions, and all good things do procede: Trusting that almighty God directing your enterprises, if you follow your godly and laudable attempts, your labors and travels herein, shall in short time obtain a happy end, with felicity and glory of all Christian people. But forasmuch as it should be a thing of great difficulty, these letters to be carried to all such places as should be expedient, we will, and of like motion and knowledge do decree that whithersoever the same shall be sent, or where soever they shall be received with the subscription of a common notary thereunto required, with the seal of any person constituted in ecelesiastical court, or such as are authorized by the ecclesiastical court, the same faith and credit to be given thereunto in judgment or elsewhere, as should be exhibited to these presents.

It shall therefore be lawful for no man to infringe or rashly to contradict this letter of our commendation, exhortation, request, donation, grant, assignation, constitution, deputation, decree, commandment, inhibition, and determination. And if any shall presume to attempt the same, he ought to know that he shall thereby incur the indignation of Almighty God and his holy Apostles, Peter and Paul.

Given at Rome, at Saint Peter's: In the year of the incarnation of our Lord M.CCCC lxx.xxiii. The fourth day of the month of May; the first year of our seat.

THE DISCOVERY OF THE MAINLAND BY THE CABOTS (1497)

I-THE ACCOUNT GIVEN BY JOHN A. DOYLE [1]

As early as the reign of Edward III, sailors from Genoa and other foreign ports had served in the English navy. The increasing confusions of Italy after the French invasion naturally tempted her seamen to transfer their skill to the rising powers of western Europe. Among such emigrants was John Cabot, a Venetian, who settled in Bristol, and then, after a return to his own country, again revisited his adopted city. Of his earlier history and personal character we know nothing. Our own records furnish nothing but the scanty outlines of his career, and the one glimpse of light which is thrown upon the living man is due to a lately discovered letter from his countryman, the Venetian ambassador. Of his son, Sebastian, we know more. He was born in Bristol, returned with his parents to Venice when three years old, and revisited England as a boy or very young man. His features, marked with the lines of thought and hardship, still live on the canvas of Holbein; and one at least of the naval chroniclers of the day writes of him in the language of warm personal affection.

In 1496 a patent was granted to John Cabot and his sons, Lewis, Sebastian, and Sancius. This patent is interesting as the earliest surviving document which connects England with the New World. It gave the patentees full authority to sail with five ships under the royal ensign, and to set up the royal banner on any newly found land, as the vassals and lieutenants of the king. They were bound on their return to sail to Bristol and to pay a royalty of one-fifth upon all clear gain. The direction of the voyage, the cargo and size of the ships, and the mode of dealing with the natives, are all left to the discretion of the commander.

Of the details of the voyage itself, so full of interest for every Englishman, we have but the scantiest knowledge. In this respect the fame of Sebastian Cabot has fared far worse than that of the great discoverer with whom alone he may be compared. We can trace Columbus through every stage of his enterprise. We seem to stand by the side of the great admiral in his difficulties, his fears, his hopes, his victory. We can almost fancy that we are sharing in his triumph when at last he sails on that mission whose end he saw but in a glass darkly, victorious over the intrigues of courtiers, the avarice of princes, and the blindness of mere worldly wisdom. Our hearts once more sink as the cowardice of his followers threatens to undo all, and the prize that had seemed won is again in danger. We feel all the intensity of suspense as night after night land is promised and the morning brings it not. When at length the goal is reached, we can almost trick ourselves with the belief that we have a part in that glory, and are of that generation by whom and for whom that mighty work was wrought.

No such halo of romantic splendor surrounds the first voyage of Sebastian Cabot. A meager extract from an old Bristol record: "In the year 1497, June 24, on St. John's Day, was Newfoundland found by Bristol men in a ship called the *Matthew*" —a few dry statements such as might be found in the note-book of any intelligent sea captain—these are all the traces of the first English voyage which reached the New World. We read in an account, probably published under the eye of Cabot himself, that on June 24, at five o'clock in the morning, he discovered that land which no man before that time had attempted, and named it Prima Vista. An adjacent island was called St. John, in commemoration of the day. A few statements about the habits of the natives and the character of the soil and the fisheries make up the whole story. We may, perhaps, infer that Cabot meant this as a report on the fitness of the place for trade and fishing, knowing that these were the points which would excite most interest in England. One entry from the privy purse expenses of Henry VII, "10£ to hym that found the new isle," is the only other record that remains to us. Columbus was received in solemn state by the sovereigns of Aragon and Castile, and was welcomed by a crowd greater than the streets of Barcelona could hold. Cabot was paid £10. The dramatic splendor of the one reception, the prosaic mercantile character of the other, represent the different tempers in which Spain and England approached the task of American discovery.

But tho our own annals give us so scanty an account of the reception of the two Cabots, the want is to some extent supplied from a foreign source. Letters are extant from the Venetian ambassador, in which he describes with just pride the enthusiasm with which his countryman was received by the people when he walked along the streets.

The next year saw Cabot again sailing with a fresh patent. Several points in it are worthy of notice. John Cabot is alone mentioned by name. From this it might be, and, indeed, has been inferred that the part played by Sebastian Cabot in the first voyage was merely secondary, and that John was the principal conductor of the first voyage, as he was by the patent designed to be of the second. He is authorized in person or by deputy to take six English ships of not more than 200 tons burden each, and to lead them to the land which he had lately discovered. There is no limitation, either of departure or return, to Bristol, and no mention is made of royalties. Probably the original provisions were still regarded as binding, except so far as rescinded or modified by the second patent.

In 1498 Sebastian Cabot sailed from Bristol with one vessel manned and victualed at the king's expense, accompanied by three ships of London, and probably some of Bristol itself. His cargo consisted of "grosse and sleighte wares," for trafficking with the natives. So scanty are the records of Cabot's two expeditions, that altho we know the geographical extent of his discoveries, yet it is impossible to assign to each voyage its proper share. We know that in one or other of them he reached 67½ degrees of north latitude, and persuaded himself that he had found the passage to Cathay. The fears, however, of his sailors, justified, perhaps, by the dangers of the north seas, withheld him from following up the enterprise. He then turned southward and coasted till he came into the latitude of 38. Of the result of the second voyage and of Sebastian Cabot's reception in England we hear nothing. He disappears for a while from English history, carrying with him the unfulfilled hope of a northwest passage, destined to revive at a later day, and then to give birth to some of the most daring exploits that have ever ennobled the names of Englishmen.

II-PETER MARTYR'S ACCOUNT [1]

These northe seas haue byn [have been] searched by one Sebastian Cabot, a Venetian borne [born], whom beinge yet but in maner an infante, his parentes caryed [carried] with them into Englande hauying [having] occasion to resorte thether [thither] for trade of marchandies [merchandise], as is the maner of the Venetians to leaue [leave] no parte of the worlde vnsearched to obteyne [obtain] richesse [riches]. He therfore furnisshed two shippes in England at his owne charges: And fyrst [first] with three hundreth men, directed his course so farre toward the northe pole, that euen [even] in the mooneth [month] of Iuly he founde monstrous heapes of Ise

[ice] swimming on the sea, and in maner continuall day lyght. Yet sawe he the lande in that tracte, free from Ise, whiche had byn [been] molten by heate of the sunne.

Thus seyng [seeing] suche heapes of Ise before hym he was enforced to tourne [turn] his sayles and folowe the weste, so coastynge styll by the shore, that he was thereby broughte so farre into the southe by reason of the lande bendynge so much southward that it was there almoste equall in latitude with the sea cauled [called] Fretum Herculeum, hauynge the north pole eleuate in maner in the same degree. He sayled lykewise in this tracte so farre towarde the weste, that he had the Ilande of Cuba [on] his lefte hande in maner in the same degree of langitude. As he traueyled [traveled] by the coastes of this greate lande (whiche he named Baccallaos) he sayth that he found the like course of the waters toward the west, but the same to runne more softely and gentelly [gently] then [than] the swifte waters whiche the Spanyardes found in their nauigations southeward.

Wherefore, it is not onely [only] more lyke to bee trewe [true], but ought also of necessitie to be concluded that betwene both the landes hetherto vnknowen, there shulde bee certeyne great open places wherby the waters shulde thus continually passe from the East into the weste: which waters I suppose to bee dryuen [driven] about the globe of the earth by the vncessaunt mouynge [moving] and impulsion of the heauens: and not to be swalowed vp [up] and cast owt [out] ageyne [again] by the breathynge of Demogorgon as sume [some] haue imagined bycause they see the seas by increase and decrease, to flowe and reflowe. Sebastian Cabot him selfe, named those landes Baccallaos, bycause that in the seas therabout he founde so great multitudes of certeyne [certain] bigge fysshes [fishes] much lyke vnto tunies [tunnies] (which th[e] inhabitantes caule [call] Baccallaos) that they sumtymes stayed his shippes. He founde also the people of those regions couered with beastes skynnes: yet not without th[e] use of reason.

He saythe [saith] also that there is greate plentie of beares in those regions, whiche vse to eate fysshe. For plungeinge thym selues [themselves] into the water where they perceue [perceive] a multitude of these fysshes to lye, they fasten theyr [their] clawes in theyr scales, and so drawe them to lande and eate them. So that (as he saith) the beares beinge thus satisfied with fysshe, are not noysom to men. He declareth further, that in many places of these regions, he sawe great plentie of laton amonge th[e] inhabitantes. Cabot is my very frende, whom I vse famylierly, and delyte [delight] to haue hym sumtymes keepe mee company in myne owne house.

For beinge cauled owte [out] of England by the commaundement of the catholyke kynge of Castile after the deathe of Henry kynge of Englande the seuenth of that name, he was made one of owre [our] counsayle and assystance as touchynge the affayres [affairs] of the newe Indies, lookynge dayely for shippes to bee furnysshed for hym to discouer this hyd secreate of nature. This vyage is appoynted to bee begunne in March in the yeare next folowynge, beinge the yeare of Chryst M.D.XVI. What shall succeade, yowre [your] holynes shalbe aduertised by my letters if god graunte me lyfe [life]. Sume of the Spanyardes denye that Cabot was the fyrst fynder of the lande of Baccallaos: And afflrme that he went not so farre westewarde. But it shall suffice to haue sayde thus much of the goulfes [gulfs] & strayghtes [straits], and of Cebastian Cabot..

THE VOYAGES OF AMERICUS VESPUCIUS (1497)

VESPUCIUS' OWN ACCOUNT [1]

We left the port of Cadiz four consort ships: and began our voyage in direct course to the Fortunate Isles, which are called to-day la gran Canaria, which are situated in the Ocean-sea at the extremity of the inhabited west, (and) set in the third climate: over which the North Pole has an elevation of 27 and a half degrees beyond their horizon: and they are 280 leagues distant from this city of Lisbon, by the wind between mezzo di and libeccio: where we remained eight days, taking in provision of water, and wood and other necessary things: and from here, having said our Pier prayers, we weighed anchor, and gave the sails to the wind, beginning our course to westward, taking one-quarter by southwest: and so we sailed on till at the end of 37 days we reached a land which we deemed to be a continent: which is distant westwardly from the isles of Canary about a thousand leagues beyond the inhabited region within the torrid zone: for we found the North Pole at an elevation of 16 degrees above its horizon, and (it was) westward, according to the shewing of our instruments, 75 degrees from the isles of Canary: whereat we anchored with our ships a league and a half from land: and we put out our boats freighted with men and arms.

We made toward the land, and before we reached it, had sight of a great number of people who were going along the shore: by which we were much rejoiced: and we observed that they were a naked race: they shewed themselves to stand in fear of us: I believe (it was) because they saw us clothed and of other appearance (than their own): they all withdrew to a hill, and for whatsoever signals we made to them of peace and of friendliness, they would not come to parley with us: so that, as the night was now coming on, and as the ships were anchored in a dangerous place, being on a rough and shelterless coast, we decided to remove from there the next day, and to go in search of some harbour or bay, where we might place our ships in safety: and we sailed with the maestrale wind, thus running along the coast with the land ever in sight, continually in our course observing people along the shore: till after having navigated for two days, we found a place sufficiently secure for the ships, and anchored half a league from land, on which we saw a very great number of people.

This same day we put to land with the boats, and sprang on shore full 40 men in good trim: and still the land's people appeared shy of converse with us, and we were unable to encourage them so much as to make them come to speak with us: and this day we laboured so greatly in giving them of our wares, such as rattles and mirrors, beads, spalline, and other trifles, that some of them took confidence and came to discourse with us: and after having made good friends with them, the night coming on, we took our leave of them and returned to the ships: and the next day when the dawn appeared we saw that there were infinite numbers of people upon the beach, and they had their women and children with them: we went ashore, and found that they were all laden with their worldly goods which are suchlike as, in its (proper) place, shall be related: and before we reached the land, many of them jumped into the sea and came swimming to receive us at a bowshot's length (from the shore), for they are very great swimmers, with as much confidence as if they had for a long time been acquainted with us: and we were pleased with this, their confidence.

For so much as we learned of their manner of life and customs, it was that they go entirely naked, as well the men as the women. They are of medium stature, very well proportioned: their flesh is of a colour that verges into red like a lion's mane: and I believe that if they went clothed, they would be as white as we: they have not any hair upon the body, except the hair of the head, which is long and black, and especially in the women, whom it renders handsome. In aspect they are not very good-looking, because they have broad faces, so that they would seem Tartar-like: they let no hair grow on their eyebrows, nor on their eyelids, nor elsewhere, except the hair of the head: for they hold hairiness to be a filthy thing: they are very light footed in walking and in running, as well the men as the women: so that a woman reeks nothing of running a league or two, as many times we saw them do: and herein they have a very great advantage over us Christians: they swim (with an expertness) beyond all belief, and the women better than the men: for we have many times found and seen them swimming two leagues out at sea without anything to rest upon. Their arms are bows and arrows very well made, save that (the arrows) are not (tipped) with iron nor any other kind of hard metal: and instead of iron they put animals' or fishes' teeth, or a spike of tough wood, with the point hardened by fire: they are sure marksmen, for they hit whatever they aim at: and in some places the women use these bows: they have other weapons, such as fire-hardened spears, and also clubs with knobs, beautifully carved.... Warfare is used amongst them, which they carry on against people not of their own language, very cruelly, without granting life to any one, except (to reserve him) for greater suffering.

Their dwellings are in common: and their houses (are) made in the style of huts, but strongly made, and constructed with very large trees, and covered over with palm-leaves, secure against storms and winds: and in some places (they are) of so great breadth and length, that in one single house we found there were 600 souls: and we saw a village of only thirteen houses where there were four thousand souls: every eight or ten years they change their habitations: and when asked why they did so: (they said it was) because of the soil, which, from its filthiness, was already unhealthy and corrupted, and that it bred aches in their bodies, which seemed to us a good reason: their riches consist of birds' plumes in many colours, or of rosaries which they make from fishbones, or of white or green stones which they put in their cheeks and in their lips and ears, and of many other things which we in no wise value: they use no trade, they neither buy nor sell. In fine, they live and are contented with that which nature gives them. The wealth that we enjoy in this our Europe and elsewhere, such as gold, jewels, pearls, and other riches, they hold as nothing: and altho they have them in their own lands, they do not labour to obtain them, nor do they value them. They are liberal in giving, for it is rarely they deny you anything, and on the other hand, liberal in asking, when they shew themselves your friends.

We decided to leave that place, and to go further on, continuously coasting the shore: upon which we made frequent descents, and held converse with a great number of people: and at the end of some days we went into a harbour where we underwent very great danger: and it pleased the Holy Ghost to save us: and it was in this wise. We landed in a harbour, where we found a village built like Venice upon the water: there were about 44 large dwellings in the form of huts erected upon very thick piles, and they had their doors or entrances in the style of drawbridges: and from each house one could pass through all, by means of the drawbridges, which stretched from house to house: and when the people thereof had seen us, they appeared to be afraid of us, and immediately drew up all the bridges: and while we were looking at this strange action, we saw coming across the sea about 22 canoes, which are a kind of boats of theirs, constructed from a single tree: which came toward our boats, as they had been surprized by our appearance and clothes, and kept wide of us: and thus remaining, we made signals to them that they should approach us, encouraging them with every token of friendliness: and seeing that they did not come, we went to them, and they did not stay for us, but made to the land, and, by signs, told us to wait, and that they should soon return: and they went to a bill in the background, and did not delay long: when they returned, they led with them 16 of their girls, and entered with these into their canoes, and came to the boats: and in each boat they put four of the girls.

That we marveled at this behavior your Magnificence can imagine how much, and they placed themselves with their canoes among our boats, coming to speak with us: insomuch that we deemed it a mark of friendliness: and while thus engaged we beheld a great number of people advance swimming toward us across the sea, who came from the houses: and as they were drawing near to us without any apprehension: just then there appeared at the doors of the houses certain old women, uttering very loud cries and tearing their hair to exhibit grief: whereby they made us suspicious, and we each betook ourselves to arms: and instantly the girls whom we had in the boats, threw themselves into the sea, and the men of the canoes drew away from us, and began with their bows to shoot arrows at us: and those who were swimming each carried a lance held, as covertly as they could, beneath the water: so that, recognizing the treachery, we engaged with them, not merely to defend ourselves, but to attack them vigorously, and we overturned with our boats any of their almadie or canoes, for so they call them, we made a slaughter (of them), and they all flung themselves into the water to swim, leaving their canoes abandoned, with considerable loss on their side, they went swimming away to the shore: there died of them about 15 or 20, and many were left wounded: and of ours 5 were wounded, and all, by the grace of God, escaped (death): we captured two of the girls and two men: and we proceeded to their houses, and entered therein, and in them all we found nothing else than two old women and a sick man: we took away from them many things, but of small value: and we would not burn their houses, because it seemed to us (as tho that would be) a burden upon our conscience: and we returned to our boats with five prisoners: and betook ourselves to the ships, and put a pair of irons on the feet of each of the captives, except the little girls: and when the night came on, the two girls and one of the men fled away in the most subtle manner possible: and the next day we decided to quit that harbour and go further onwards.

We proceeded continuously skirting the coast, (until) we had sight of another tribe distant perhaps some 80 leagues from the former tribe: and we found them very different in speech and customs: we resolved to cast anchor, and went ashore with the boats, and we saw on the beach a great number of people amounting probably to 4,000 souls: and when we had reached the shore, they did not stay for us, but betook themselves to flight through the forests, abandoning their things: we jumped on land, and took a pathway that led to the forest: and at the distance of a bow-shot we found their tents, where they had made very large fires, and two (of them) were cooking their victuals, and roasting several animals, and fish of many kinds:

where we saw that they were roasting a certain animal which seemed to be a serpent, save that it had no wings, and was in its appearance so loathsome that we marveled much at its savageness:

Thus went we on through their houses, or rather tents, and found many of those serpents alive, and they were tied by the feet and had a cord around their snouts, so that they could not open their mouths, as is done (in Europe) with mastiff-dogs so that they may not bite: they were of such savage aspect that none of us dared to take one away, thinking that they were poisonous: they are of the bigness of a kid, and in length an ell and a half: their feet are long and thick, and armed with big claws: they have a hard skin, and are of various colors: they have the muzzle and face of a serpent: and from their snouts there rises a crest like a saw which extends along the middle of the back as far as the tip of the tail: in fine we deemed them to be serpents and venomous, and (nevertheless, those people) ate them.

This land is very populous, and full of inhabitants, and of numberless rivers, (and) animals: few (of which) resemble ours, excepting lions, panthers, stags, pigs, goats, and deer: and even these have some dissimilarities of form: they have no horses nor mules, nor, saving your reverence, asses nor dogs, nor any kind of sheep or oxen: but so numerous are the other animals which they have, and all are savage, and of none do they make use for their service, that they could not he counted. What shall we say of others (such as) birds? which are so numerous, and of so many kinds, and of such various-coloured plumages, that it is a marvel to behold them. The soil is very pleasant and fruitful, full of immense woods and forests: and it is always green, for the foliage never drops off. The fruits are so many that they are numberless and entirely different from ours. This land is within the torrid zone, close to or just under the parallel described by the Tropic of Cancer: where the pole of the horizon has an elevation of 23 degrees, at the extremity of the second climate. Many tribes came to see us, and wondered at our faces and our whiteness: and they asked us whence we came: and we gave them to understand that we had come from heaven, and that we were going to see the world, and they believed it. In this land we placed baptismal fonts, and an infinite (number of) people were baptized, and they called us in their language Carabi, which means men of great wisdom.

A BATTLE WITH THE INDIANS (1497)

AS DESCRIBED BY AMERICUS VESPUCIUS [1]

Desiring to depart upon our voyage natives made complaint to us how at certain times of the year there came from over the sea to this their land, a race of people very cruel, and enemies of theirs: and (who) by means of treachery or of violence slew many of them, and ate them: and some they made captives, and carried them away to their houses, or country: and how they could scarcely contrive to defend themselves from them, making signs to us that (those) were an island-people and lived out in the sea about a hundred leagues away: and so piteously did they tell us this that we believed them: and we promised to avenge them of so much wrong: and they remained overjoyed herewith: and many of them offered to come along with us, but we did not wish to take them for many reasons, save that we took seven of them, on condition that they should come (*i.e.*, return home) afterward in (their own) canoes because we did not desire to be obliged to take them back to their country: and they were contented: and so we departed from those people, leaving them very friendly toward us: and having repaired our ships, and sailing for seven days out to sea between northeast and east: and at the end of the seven days we came upon the islands, which were many, some (of them) inhabited, and others deserted: and we anchored at one of them: where we saw a numerous people who called it Iti: and having manned our boats with strong crews, and (taken ammunition for) three cannon shots in each, we made for land: where we found (assembled) about 400 men, and many women, and all naked like the former (peoples).

They were of good bodily presence, and seemed right warlike men: for they were armed with their weapons, which are bows, arrows, and lances: and most of them had square wooden targets: and bore them in such wise that they did not impede the drawing of the bow: and when we had come with our boats to about a bowshot of the land, they all sprang into the water to shoot their arrows at us, and to prevent us from leap-lug upon shore: and they all had their bodies painted of various colours, and (were) plumed with feathers: and the interpreters who were with us told us that when (those) displayed themselves so painted and plumed, it was to betoken that they wanted to fight: and so much did they persist in preventing us from landing, that we were compelled to play with our artillery: and when they heard the explosion, and saw one of them fall dead, they all drew back to the land: wherefore, forming our council, we resolved that 42 of our men should spring on shore, and, if they waited for us, fight them: thus having leaped to land with our weapons, they advanced toward us, and we fought for about an hour, for we had but little advantage of them, except that our arbalasters and gunners killed some of them, and they wounded certain of our men. This was because they did not stand to receive us within reach of lance-thrust or sword-blow: and so much vigor did we put forth at last, that we came to sword-play, and when they tasted our weapons, they betook themselves to flight through the mountains and the forests, and left us conquerors of the field with many of them dead and a good number wounded.

We took no other pains to pursue them, because we were very weary, and we returned to our ships, with so much gladness on the part of the seven men who had come with us that they could not contain themselves (for joy): and when the next day arrived, we beheld coming across the land a great number of people, with signals of battle, continually sounding horns, and various other instruments which they use in their wars: and all (of them) painted and feathered, so that it was a very strange sight to behold them: wherefore all the ships held council, and it was resolved that since this people desired hostility with us, we should proceed to encounter them and try by every means to make them friends: in case they would not have our friendship, that we should treat them as foes, and so many of them as we might be able to capture should all be our slaves: and having armed ourselves as best we could, we advanced toward the shore, and they sought not to hinder us from landing, I believe, from fear of the cannons: and we jumped on land, 57 men in four squadrons, each one (consisting of) a captain and his company: and we came to blows with them.

After a long battle many of them (were) slain, we put them to flight, and pursued them to a village, having made about 250 of them captives, and we burnt the village, and returned to our ships with victory and 250 prisoners, leaving many of them dead and wounded, and of ours there were no more than one killed, and 22 wounded, who all escaped (*i.e.*, recovered), God be thanked. We arranged our departure, and seven men, of whom five were wounded, took an island-canoe, and with seven prisoners that we gave them, four women and three men, returned to their (own) country full of gladness, wondering at our strength: and we thereon made sail for Spain with 222 captive slaves: and reached the port of Calis (Cadiz) on the 15th day of October, 1498, where we were well received and sold our slaves. Such is what befell me, most noteworthy, in this my first voyage.

THE FIRST ACCOUNT OF AMERICA PRINTED IN ENGLISH (1511) [1]

Of the newe landes and of ye people founde by the messengers of the kynge of Portyugale named Emanuel. of the R. [5] Dyners Nacyons crystened. Of Pope John and his landes and of the costely keyes and wonders molo dyes that in that lande is.

Here aforetymes [formerly] in the yere of our Lorde god. M.CCCC.xcvi. [1496] and so be we with shyppes of Lusseboene [Lisbon] sayled oute of Portyugale thorough the commaundement of the Kynge Emanuel. So haue we had our vyage. For by fortune ylandes ouer the great see with great charge and daunger so haue we at the laste founde oon lordshyp where we sayled well. ix.C. [900] mylee [mile] by the cooste of Selandes there we at ye laste went a lande but that lande is not nowe knowen for there haue no masters wryten thereof nor it knowethe and it is named Armenica [America] there we sawe meny wonders of beestes and fowles yat [that] we haue neuer seen before the people of this lande haue no kynge nor lorde nor theyr god But all thinges is comune.... the men and women haue on theyr heed necke Armes Knees and fete all with feders [feathers] bounden for their bewtynes [beauty] and fayrenes.

These folke lyuen [live] lyke bestes without any resenablenes.... And they etc [eat] also on[e] a nother. The man etethe [eateth] his wyfe, his chylderne as we also haue seen, and they hange also the bodyes or persons fleeshe in the smoke as men do with vs swynes fleshe. And that lande is ryght full of folke for they lyue commonly. iii.C. [300] yere and more as with sykenesse they dye nat they take much fysshe for they can goen vnder the water and fe[t]che so the fysshes out of the water. and they werre [war] also on[e] vpon a nother for the olde men brynge the yonge men thereto that they gather a great company thereto of towe [two] partyes and come the on[e] ayene [against] the other to the felde or bateyll [battle] and slee [slay] on[e] the other with great hepes [heaps]. And nowe holdeth the fylde [field] they take the other prysoners And they brynge them to deth and ete them and as the deed [dead] is eten then fley [flay] they the rest. And they been [are] than [then] eten also or otherwyse lyue they longer tymes and many yeres more than other people for they haue costely spyces and rotes [roots] where they them selfe recouer with and hele [heal] them as they be seke [sick].

THE DISCOVERY OF FLORIDA BY PONCE DE LEON (1512)

PARKMAN'S ACCOUNT [1]

Toward the close of the fifteenth century Spain achieved her final triumph over the infidels of Granada, and made her name glorious through all generations by the discovery of America. The religious zea and romantic daring which a long course of Moorish wars had called forth were now exalted to redoubled fervor. Every ship from the New World came freighted with marvels which put the fictions of chivalry to shame; and to the Spaniard of that day America was a region of wonder and mystery, of vague and magnificent promise. Thither adventurers hastened, thirsting for glory and for gold, and often mingling the enthusiasm of the crusader and the valor of the knight-errant with the bigotry of inquisitors and the rapacity of pirates. They roamed over land and sea; they climbed unknown mountains, surveyed unknown oceans, pierced the sultry intricacies of tropical forests; while from year to year and from day to day new wonders were unfolded, new islands and archipelagoes, new regions of gold and pearl, and barbaric empires of more than Oriental wealth. The extravagance of hope and the fever of adventure knew no bounds. Nor is it surprizing that amid such waking marvels the imagination should run wild in romantic dreams; that between the possible and the impossible the line of distinction should be but faintly drawn, and that men should be found ready to stake life and honor in pursuit of the most insane fantasies.

Such a man was the veteran cavalier Juan Ponce de Leon. Greedy of honors and of riches, he embarked at Porto Rico with three brigantines, bent on schemes of discovery. But that which gave the chief stimulus to his enterprise was a story, current among the Indians of Cuba and Hispaniola, that on the island of Bimini, said to be one of the Bahamas, there was a fountain of such virtue, that, bathing in its waters, old men resumed their youth. [2] It was said, moreover, that on a neighboring shore might be found a river gifted with the same beneficent property, and believed by some to be no other than the Jordan. Ponce de Leon found the island of Bimini, but not the fountain. Farther westward, in the latitude of 30 degrees and 8 minutes, he approached an unknown land, which he named Florida, and, steering southward, explored its coast as far as the extreme point of the peninsula, when, after some further explorations, he retraced his course to Porto Rico.

Ponce de Leon had not regained his youth, but his active spirit was unsubdued. Nine years later he attempted to plant a colony in Florida; the Indians attacked him fiercely; he was mortally wounded, and died soon afterward in Cuba.

The voyages of Garay and Vasquez de Ayllon threw new light on the discoveries of Ponce, and the general outline of the coasts of Florida became known to the Spaniards. Meanwhile, Cortes had conquered Mexico, and the fame of that iniquitous but magnificent exploit rang through all Spain. Many an impatient cavalier burned to achieve a kindred fortune. To the excited fancy of the Spaniards the unknown land of Florida seemed the seat of surpassing wealth, and Pamphilo de Narvaez essayed to possess himself of its fancied treasures. Landing on its shores, and proclaiming destruction to the Indians unless they acknowledged the sovereignty of the Pope and the Emperor, he advanced into the forests with three hundred men. Nothing could exceed their sufferings. Nowhere could they find the gold they came to seek. The village of Appalache, where they hoped to gain a rich booty, offered nothing but a few mean wigwams. The horses gave out, and the famished soldiers fed upon their flesh. The men sickened, and the Indians unceasingly harassed their march. At length, after 280 leagues of wandering, they found themselves on the northern shore of the Gulf of Mexico, and desperately put to sea in such crazy boats as their skill and means could construct. Cold, disease, famine, thirst, and the fury of the waves melted them away. Narvaez himself perished, and of his wretched followers no more than four escaped, reaching by land, after years of vicissitude, the Christian settlements of New Spain.

The interior of the vast country then comprehended under the name of Florida still remained unexplored. The Spanish voyager, as his caravel plowed the adjacent seas, might give full scope to his imagination, and dream that beyond the long, low margin of forest which bounded his horizon lay hid a rich harvest for some future conqueror; perhaps a second

Mexico, with its royal palace and sacred pyramids, or another Cuzco, with the temple of the Sun, encircled with a frieze of gold.

THE DISCOVERY OF THE PACIFIC BY BALBOA (1513)

THE ACCOUNT BY MANUEL JOSE QUINTANA [1]

Careta [2] had for a neighbor a cacique called by some Comogre, by others Panquiaco, chief of about ten thousand Indians, among whom were 3,000 warriors. Having heard of the valor and enterprise of the Castilians, this chief desired to enter into treaty and friendship with them; and a principal Indian, a dependent of Careta, having presented himself as the agent in this friendly overture, Vasco Nuñez, anxious to profit by the opportunity of securing such an ally, went with his followers to visit Comogre....

Balboa was transported by the prospect of glory and fortune which opened before him; he believed himself already at the gates of the East Indies, which was the desired object of the government and the discoverers of that period; he resolved to return in the first place to the Darien to raise the spirits of his companions with these brilliant hopes, and to make all possible preparations for realizing them. He remained, nevertheless, yet a few days with the caciques; and so strict was the friendship he had contracted with them that they and their families were baptized, Careta taking in baptism the name of Fernando, and Comogre that of Carlos. Balboa then returned to the Darien, rich in the spoils of Ponca, rich in the presents of his friends, and still richer in the golden hopes which the future offered him.

At this time, and after an absence of six months, arrived the magistrate Valdivia, with a vessel laden with different stores; he brought likewise great promises of abundant aid in provisions and men. The succors, however, which Valdivia brought were speedily consumed; their seed, destroyed in the ground by storms and floods, promised them no resource whatever; and they returned to their usual necessitous state. Balboa then consented to their extending their incursions to more distant lands, as they had already wasted and ruined the immediate environs of Antigua, and he sent Valdivia to Spain to apprize the admiral of the clew he had gained to the South Sea, and the reported wealth of these regions.

He discoursed with and animated his companions, selected 190 of the best armed, and disposed, and, with a thousand Indians of labor, a few bloodhounds, and sufficient provisions, took his way by the sierras toward the dominion of Ponca. That chief had fled, but Balboa, who had adopted the policy most convenient to him, desired to bring him to an amicable agreement, and, to that end, dispatched after him some Indians of peace, who advised him to return to his capital and to fear nothing from the Spaniards. He was persuaded, and met with a kind reception; he presented some gold, and received in return some glass beads and other toys and trifles. The Spanish captains then solicited guides and men of labor for his journey over the sierras, which the cacique bestowed willingly, adding provisions in great abundance, and they parted friends.

His passage into the domain of Quarequa was less pacific; whose chief, Torecha, jealous of this invasion, and terrified by the events which had occurred to his neighbors, was disposed and prepared to receive the Castilians with a warlike aspect. A swarm of ferocious Indians, armed in their usual manner, rushed into the road and began a wordy attack upon the strangers, asking them what brought them there, what they sought for, and threatening him with perdition if they advanced. The Spaniards, reckless of their bravados, proceeded, nevertheless, and then the chief placed himself in front of his tribe, drest in a cotton mantle and followed by the principal lords, and with more intrepidity than fortune, gave the signal for combat. The Indians commenced the assault with loud cries and great impetuosity, but, soon terrified by the explosions of the crossbows and muskets, they were easily destroyed or put to flight by the men and bloodhounds who rushed upon them. The chief and 600 men were left dead on the spot, and the Spaniards, having smoothed away that obstacle, entered the town, which they spoiled of all the gold and valuables it possest. Here, also, they found a brother of the cacique and other Indians, who were dedicated to the abominations before glanced at; fifty of these wretches were torn to pieces by the dogs, and not without the consent and approbation of the Indians. The district was, by these examples, rendered so pacific and so submissive that Balboa left all his sick there, dismissed the guides given him by Ponca, and, taking fresh ones, pursued his road over the heights.

The tongue of land which divides the two Americas is not, at its utmost width, above eighteen leagues, and in some parts becomes narrowed a little more than seven. And, altho from the port of Careta to the point toward which the course of the Spaniards was directed was only altogether six days' journey, yet they consumed upon it twenty; nor is this extraordinary. The great cordillera of sierras which from north to south crosses the new continent, a bulwark against the impetuous assaults of the Pacific Ocean, crosses also the Isthmus of Darien, or, as may be more properly said, composes it wholly, from the wrecks of the rocky summits which have been detached from the adjacent lands; and the discoverers, therefore, were obliged to open their way through difficulties and dangers which men of iron alone could have fronted and overcome. Sometimes they had to penetrate through thick entangled woods, sometimes to cross lakes, where men and burdens perished miserably; then a rugged hill presented itself before them; and next, perhaps, a deep and yawning precipice to descend; while, at every step, they were opposed by deep and rapid rivers, passable only by means of frail barks, or slight and trembling bridges; from time to time they had to make their way through opposing Indians, who, tho always conquered, were always to be dreaded; and, above all, came the failure of provisions—which formed an aggregate, with toil, anxiety, and danger, such as was sufficient to break down bodily strength and depress the mind....

At length the Quarequanos, who served as guides, showed them, at a distance, the height from whose summit the desired sea might be discovered. Balboa immediately commanded his squadron to halt, and proceeded alone to the top of the mountain; on reaching it he cast an anxious glance southward, and the Austral Ocean broke upon his sight. [3] Overcome with joy and wonder, he fell on his knees, extending his arms toward the sea, and with tears of delight, offered thanks to heaven for having destined him to this mighty discovery. He immediately made a sign to his companions to ascend, and, pointing to the magnificent spectacle extended before them, again prostrated himself in fervent thanksgiving to God. The rest followed his example, while the astonished Indians were extremely puzzled to understand so sudden and general an effusion of wonder and gladness. Hannibal on the summit of the Alps, pointing out to his soldiers the delicious plains of Italy, did not appear, according to the ingenious comparison of a contemporary writer, either more transported or more arrogant than the

Spanish chief, when, risen from the ground, he recovered the speech of which sudden joy had deprived him, and thus addrest his Castilians: "You behold before you, friends, the object of all our desires and the reward of all our labors. Before you roll the waves of the sea which has been announced to you, and which no doubt encloses the immense riches we have heard of. You are the first who have reached these shores and these waves; yours are their treasures, yours alone the glory of reducing these immense and unknown regions to the dominion of our King and to the light of the true religion. Follow me, then, faithful as hitherto, and I promise you that the world shall not hold your equals in wealth and glory."

All embraced him joyfully and all promised to follow whithersoever he should lead. They quickly cut down a great tree, and, stripping it of its branches, formed a cross from it, which they fixt in a heap of stones found on the spot from whence they first descried the sea. The names of the monarchs of Castile were engraven on the trunks of the trees, and with shouts and acclamations they descended the sierra and entered the plain.

They arrived at some bohios, which formed the population of a chief, called Chiapes, who had prepared to defend the pass with arms. The noise of the muskets and the ferocity of the war-dogs dispersed them in a moment, and they fled, leaving many captives; by these and by their Quarequano guides, the Spaniards sent to offer Chiapes secure peace and friendship if he would come to them, or otherwise the ruin and extermination of his town and his fields. Persuaded by them, the cacique came and placed himself in the hands of Balboa, who treated him with much kindness. He brought and distributed gold and received in exchange beads and toys, with which he was so diverted that he no longer thought of anything but contenting and conciliating the strangers. There Vasco Nuñez sent away the Quarequanos, and ordered that the sick, who had been left in their land, should come and join him. In the meanwhile he sent Francisco Pizarro, Juan de Ezcarag, and Alonzo Martin to discover the shortest roads by which the sea might be reached. It was the last of these who arrived first at the coast, and, entering a canoe which chanced to lie there, and pushing it into the waves, let it float a little while, and, after pleasing himself with having been the first Spaniard who entered the South Sea, returned to seek Balboa.

Balboa with twenty-six men descended to the sea, and arrived at the coast early in the evening of the 29th of that month; they all seated themselves on the shore and awaited the tide, which was at that time on the ebb. At length it returned in its violence to cover the spot where they were; then Balboa, in complete armor, lifting his sword in one hand, and in the other a banner on which was painted an image of the Virgin Mary with the arms of Castile at her feet, raised it, and began to march into the midst of the waves, which reached above his knees, saying in a loud voice: "Long live the high and mighty sovereigns of Castile! Thus in their names do I take possession of these seas and regions; and if any other prince, whether Christian or infidel, pretends any right to them, I am ready and resolved to oppose him, and to assert the just claims of my sovereigns."

The whole band replied with acclamations to the vow of their captain, and exprest themselves determined to defend, even to death, their acquisition against all the potentates in the world; they caused this act to be confirmed in writing, by the notary of the expedition, Andres de Valderrabano; the anchorage in which it was solemnized was called the Gulf of San Miguel, the event happening on that day.

THE VOYAGE OF MAGELLAN TO THE PACIFIC (1520)

JOHN FISKE'S ACCOUNT [1]

Our chief source of information for the events of the voyage is the journal kept by a gentleman from Vicenza, the Chevalier Antonio Pigafetta, who obtained permission to accompany the expedition, "for to see the marvels of the ocean." After leaving the Canaries on the 3d of October, the armada ran down toward Sierra Leone, and was becalmed, making only three leagues in three weeks. Then "the upper air burst into life" and the frail ships were driven along under bare poles, now and then dipping their yard-arms. During a month of this dreadful weather, the food and water grew scarce, and the rations were diminished. The spirit of mutiny began to show itself. The Spanish captains whispered among the crews that this man from Portugal had not their interests at heart, and was not loyal to the Emperor. Toward the captain-general their demeanor grew more and more insubordinate; and Cartagena one day, having come on board the flag-ship, faced him with threats and insults. To his astonishment, Magellan promptly collared him, and sent him, a prisoner in irons, on board the *Victoria* (whose captain was unfortunately also one of the traitors), while the command of the *San Antonio* was given to another officer. This example made things quiet for the moment.

On the 29th of November they reached the Brazilian coast near Pernambuco; and on the 11th of January they arrived at the mouth of La Plata, which they investigated sufficiently to convince them that it was a river's mouth, and not a strait. Three weeks were consumed in this work. This course through February and March along the coast of Patagonia was marked by incessant and violent storms; and the cold became so intense that, finding a sheltered harbor with plenty of fish at Port St. Julian, they chose it for winter quarters and anchored there on the last day of March. On the next day, which was Easter Sunday, the mutiny that so long had smoldered broke out in all its fury.

The hardships of the voyage had thus far been what stanch seamen called unusually severe, and it was felt that they had done enough. No one except Vespucius and Jaques had ever approached so near to the South Pole; and if they had not yet found a strait, it was doubtless because there was none to find. The rations of bread and wine were becoming very short, and common prudence demanded that they should return to Spain. If their voyage was practically a failure, it was not their fault; there was ample excuse in the frightful storms they had suffered and the dangerous strains that had been put upon their worn-out ships. Such was the general feeling, but when exprest to Magellan it fell upon deaf ears. No excuses, nothing but performance, would serve his turn; for him hardships were made only to be despised, and dangers to be laughed at: and, in short, go on they must, until a strait was found or the end of that continent reached. Then they would doubtless find an open way to the Moluccas; and while he held out hopes of rich rewards for all he appealed to their pride as Castilians. For the inflexible determination of this man was not embittered by harshness, and he could wield as well as any one the language that soothes and persuades.

At length, on the 24th of August, with the earliest symptoms of spring weather, the ships, which had been carefully overhauled and repaired, proceeded on their way. Violent storms harassed them, and it was not until the 21st of October (St. Ursala's day) that they reached the headland still known as Cape Virgins. Passing beyond Dungeness, they entered a large open bay, which some hailed as the long-sought strait, while others averred that no passage would be found there. "It was," says Pigafetta, "in Eden's bredth. On both the sydes of this strayght are Magellanus, beinge in sum place C.x. leagues in length: and in breadth sumwhere very large and in other places lyttle more than halfe a leaque in bredth. On both the sydes of this strayght are great and hygh mountaynes couered with snowe, beyonde the whiche is the enteraunce into the sea of Sur.... Here one of the shyppes stole away priuilie and returned into Spayne." More than five weeks were consumed in passing through the strait, and among its labyrinthine twists and half-hidden bays there was ample opportunity for desertion. As advanced reconnoissances kept reporting the water as deep and salt, the conviction grew that the strait was found, and then the question once more arose whether it would not be best to go back to Spain, satisfied with this discovery, since with all these wretched delays the provisions were again running short. Magellan's answer, uttered in measured and quiet tones, was simply that he would go on and do his work "if he had to eat the leather off the ship's yards." Upon the *San Antonio* there had always been a large proportion of the malcontents, and the chief pilot, Estevan Gomez, having been detailed for duty on that ship, lent himself to their purposes. The captain, Mesquita, was again seized and put in irons, a new captain was chosen by the mutineers, and Gomez piloted the ship back to Spain, where they arrived after a voyage of six months, and screened themselves for a while by lying about Magellan.

As for that commander, in Richard Eden's words, "when the capitayne Magalianes was past the strayght and sawe the way open to the other mayne sea, he was so gladde thereof that for joy the teares fell from his eyes, and named the point of the lande from whense he fyrst sawe that sea Capo Desiderato. Supposing that the shyp which stole away had byn loste, they erected a crosse uppon the top of a hyghe hyll to direct their course in the straight yf it were theyr chaunce to coome that way." The broad expanse of waters before him seemed so pleasant to Magellan, after the heavy storms through which he had passed, that he called it by the name it still bears, Pacific. But the worst hardships were still before him. Once more a sea of darkness must be crossed by brave hearts sickening with hope deferred. If the mid-Atlantic waters had been strange to Columbus and his men, here before Magellan's people all was thrice unknown.

"They were the first that ever burst
Into that silent sea";

and as they sailed month after month over the waste of waters, the huge size of our planet began to make itself felt. Until after the middle of December they kept a northward course, near the coast of the continent, running away from the antarctic cold. Then northwesterly and westerly courses were taken, and on the 24th of January, 1521, a small wooded islet was found in water where the longest plummet-lines failed to reach bottom. Already the voyage since issuing from the strait was nearly twice as long as that of Columbus in 1492 from the Canaries to Guanahani. From the useless island, which they called San Pablo, a further run of eleven days brought them to another uninhabited rock, which they called Tiburones, from the quantity of sharks observed in the neighborhood. There was neither food, nor water to be had there, and a voyage of unknown duration, in reality not less than 5,000 English miles, was yet to be accomplished before a trace of land was again to greet their yearning gaze. Their sufferings may best be told in the quaint and touching words in which Shakespeare read them:

"And hauynge in this tyme consumed all theyr bysket and other vyttayles, they fell into such necessitie that they were inforced to eate the pouder that remayned therof beinge now full of woormes.... Theyre freshe water was also putrifyed and become yelow. They dyd eate skynnes and pieces of lether which were foulded abowt certeyne great ropes of the shyps. But these skynnes being made verye harde by reason of the soonne, rayne, and wynde, they hunge them by a corde in the sea for the space of foure or fiue dayse to mollifie them, and sodde them, and eate them. By reason of this famen and vnclene feedynge, summe of theyr gummes grewe so ouer theyr teethe [a symptom of scurvy], that they dyed miserably for hunger. And by this occasion dyed xix. men, and ... besyde these that dyed, xxv. or xxx. were so sicke that they were not able to doo any seruice with theyr handes or arms for feeblenesse: So that was in maner none without sum disease. In three monethes and xx. dayes, they sayled foure thousande leaques in one goulfe by the sayde sea cauled Paciflcum (that is) peaceable, whiche may well bee so cauled forasmuch as in all this tyme hauyng no syght of any lande, they had no misfortune of wynde or any other tempest.... So that in fine, if god of his mercy had not gyuen them good wether, it was necessary that in this soo greate a sea they shuld all haue dyed for hunger. Whiche neuertheless they escaped soo hardely, that it may bee doubted whether euer the like viage may be attempted with so goode successe."

One would gladly know—albeit Pigafetta's journal and the still more laconic pilot's logbook leave us in the dark on this point—how the ignorant and suffering crews interpreted this everlasting stretch of sea, vaster, said Maximilian Transylvanus, "than the human mind could conceive." To them it may well have seemed that the theory of a round and limited earth was wrong after all, and that their infatuated commander was leading them out into the fathomless abysses of space, with no welcoming shore beyond. But that heart of triple bronze, we may be sure, did not flinch. The situation had got beyond the point where mutiny could be suggested as a remedy. The very desperateness of it was all in Magellan's favor; for so far away had they come from the known world that retreat meant certain death. The only chance of escape lay in pressing forward. At last, on the 6th of March, they came upon islands inhabited by savages ignorant of the bow and arrow, but expert in handling their peculiar light boats. Here the dreadful sufferings were ended, for they found plenty of fruit and fresh vegetables, besides meat. The people were such eager and pertinacious thieves that their islands received the name by which they are still known, the Islas de Ladrones, or isles of robbers.

On the 16th of March the three ships arrived at the islands which some years afterward were named Philippines, after Philip II of Spain. Tho these were islands unvisited by Europeans, yet Asiatic traders from Siam and Sumatra, as well as from China, were to be met there, and it was thus not long before Magellan became aware of the greatness of his triumph. He had passed the meridian of the Moluccas, and knew that these islands lay to the southward within an easy sail. He had accomplished the circumnavigation of the earth through its unknown portion, and the remainder of his route lay through seas already traversed. An erroneous calculation of longitudes confirmed him in the belief that the Moluccas, as well as the Philippines, properly belonged to Spain. Meanwhile in these Philippines of themselves he had discovered a region of no small commercial importance. But his brief tarry in these interesting islands had fatal results; and in the very hour of victory the conqueror perished, slain in a fight with the natives, the reason of which we can understand only by considering the close complication of commercial and political interests with religious notions so common in that age....

Meanwhile, on the 16th of May, the little *Victoria*, with starvation and scurvy already thinning the ranks, with foretopmast gone by the board and fore-yard badly sprung, cleared the Cape of Good Hope, and thence was borne on the strong and friendly current up to the equator, which she crossed on the 8th of June. Only fifty years since Santarem and Escobar, first of Europeans, had crept down that coast and crossed it. Into that glorious half-century what a world of suffering and achievement had been crowded! Dire necessity compelled the *Victoria* to stop at the Cape Verde Islands. Her people sought safety in deceiving the Portuguese with the story that they were returning from a voyage in Atlantic waters only, and thus they succeeded in buying food. But while this was going on, as a boat-load of thirteen men had been sent ashore for rice, some silly tongue, loosened by wine, in the head of a sailor who had cloves to sell, babbled the perilous secret of Magellan and the Moluccas. The thirteen were at once arrested, and a boat called upon the *Victoria*, with direful threats, to surrender; but she quickly stretched every inch of her canvas and got away. This was on the 18th of July, and eight weeks of ocean remained. At last, on the 6th of September—the thirtieth anniversary of the day when Columbus weighed anchor for Cipango—the *Victoria* sailed into the Guadalquivir, with eighteen gaunt and haggard survivors to tell the proud story of the first circumnavigation of the earth.

The voyage thus ended was doubtless the greatest feat of navigation that has ever been performed, and nothing can be imagined that would surpass it except a journey to some other planet. It has not the unique historic position of the first voyage of Columbus, which brought together two streams of human life that had been disjoined since the glacial period.

But as an achievement in ocean navigation that voyage of Columbus sinks into insignificance by the side of it; and when the earth was a second time encompassed by the greatest English sailor of his age, [2] the advance in knowledge, as well as the different route chosen, had much reduced the difficulty of the performance. When we consider the frailness of the ships, the immeasurable, extent of the unknown, the mutinies that were prevented or quelled, and the hardships that were endured, we can have no hesitation in speaking of Magellan as the prince of navigators. Nor can we ever fail to admire the simplicity and purity of that devoted life, in which there is nothing that seeks to be hidden or explained away.

THE DISCOVERY OF NEW YORK HARBOR BY VERAZZANO (1524)

VERAZZANO'S OWN ACCOUNT [1]

Having remained in this place [2] three days, anchored off the coast, we decided on account of the scarcity of ports to depart, always skirting the shore, which we baptized Arcadia on account of the beauty of the trees.

In Arcadia we found a man who came to the shore to see what people we were: who stood hesitating and ready to fight. Watching us, he did not permit himself to be approached. He was handsome, nude, with hair fastened back in a knot, of olive color.

We were about XX [in number], ashore, and coaxing him, he approached to within about two fathoms, showing a burning stick as if to offer us fire. And we made fire with powder and flint and steel, and he trembled all over with terror, and we fired a shot. He stopt as if astonished, and prayed, worshiping like a monk, lifting his finger toward the sky, and pointing to the ship and the sea he appeared to bless us.

Toward the north and east, navigating by daylight and casting anchor at night, we followed a coast very green with forests, but without ports, and with some charming promontories and small rivers. We baptized the coast "di Lorenna" on account of the Cardinal; the first promontory "Lanzone," the second "Bonivetto," the largest river "Vandoma" and a small mountain which stands by the sea "di S. Polo" on account of the count.

At the end of a hundred leagues we found a very agreeable situation located within two small prominent hills, in the midst of which flowed to the sea a very great river, which was deep within the mouth; and from the sea to the hills of that [place] with the rising of the tides, which we found eight feet, any laden ship might have passed. On account of being anchored off the coast in good shelter, we did not wish to adventure in without knowledge of the entrances. We were with the small boat, entering the said river [3] to the land, which we found much populated. The people, almost like the others, clothed with the feathers of birds of various colors, came toward us joyfully, uttering very great exclamations of admiration, showing us where we could land with the boat more safely. We entered said river, within the land, about half a league, where we saw it made a very beautiful lake with a circuit of about three leagues; through which they [the Indians] went, going from one and another part to the number of XXX of their little barges, with innumerable people, who passed from one shore and the other in order to see us. In an instant, as is wont to happen in navigation, a gale of unfavorable wind blowing in from the sea, we were forced to return to the ship, leaving the said land with much regret because of its commodiousness and beauty, thinking it was not without some properties of value, all of its hills showing indications of minerals. We called it Angoleme from the principality which thou attainedst in lesser fortune, and the bay which that land makes called Santa Margarita [4] from the name of thy sister who vanquished the other matrons of modesty and art.

The anchor raised, sailing toward the east, as thus the land turned, having traveled LXXX leagues always in sight of it, we discovered an island triangular in form, distant ten leagues from the continent, in size like the island of Rhodes, full of hills, covered with trees, much populated [judging] by the continuous fires along all the surrounding shore which we saw they made. We baptized it Aloysia, in the name of your most illustrious mother; [5] not anchoring there on account of the unfavorableness of the weather.

We came to another land, distant from the island XV leagues, where we found a very beautiful port, [6] and before we entered it, we saw about XX barges of the people who came with various cries of wonder round about the ship. Not approaching nearer than fifty paces, they halted, looking at the edifice [*i.e.*, the ship], our figures and clothes; then all together they uttered a loud shout, signifying that they were glad. Having reassured them somewhat, imitating their gestures, they came so near that we threw them some little bells and mirrors and many trinkets, having taken which, regarding them with laughter, they entered the ship confidently. There were among them two Kings, of as good stature and form as it would be possible to tell; the first of about XXXX years, the other a young man of XXIIII years, the clothing of whom was thus: the older had on his nude body a skin of a stag, artificially adorned like a damask with various embroideries; the head bare, the hair turned back with various bands, at the neck a broad chain ornamented with many stones of diverse colors. The young man was almost in the same style.

This is the most beautiful people and the most civilized in customs that we have found in this navigation. They excel us in size; they are of bronze color, some inclining more to whiteness, others to tawny color; the face sharply cut, the hair long and black, upon which they bestow the greatest study in adorning it; the eyes black and alert, the bearing kind and gentle, imitating much the ancient [manner]. Of the other parts of the body I will not speak to Your Majesty, having all the proportions which belong to every well-built man. Their women are of the same beauty and charm; very graceful; of comely mien and agreeable aspect; of habits and behavior as much according to womanly custom as pertains to human nature; they go nude with only one skin of the stag embroidered like the men, and some wear on the arms very rich skins of the lynx; the head bare, with various arrangements of braids, composed of their own hair, which hang on one side and the other of the breast. Some use other hair-arrangements like the women of Egypt and of Syria use, and these are they who are advanced in age and are joined in wedlock.

They have in the ears various pendant trinkets as the orientals are accustomed to have, the men like the women, among which we saw many plates wrought from copper, by whom it is prized more than gold; which, on account of its color, they do not esteem; wherefore among all it is held by them more worthless; on the other hand rating blue and red above any other. That which they were given by us which they most valued were little bells, blue crystals and other trinkets to place in the ears and on the neck. They did not prize cloth of silk and of gold, nor even of other kind, nor did they care to have them; likewise with metals like steel and iron; for many times showing them our arms they did not conceive admiration for them nor ask for them, only examining the workmanship. They did the same with the mirrors; suddenly looking at them, they refused them, laughing. They are very liberal, so much so that all which they have they give away. We formed a great friendship with them, and one day, before we had entered with the ship in the port, remaining on account of the unfavorable weather conditions anchored a league at sea, they came in great numbers in their little barges to the ship, having painted and decked the face with various colors, showing to us it was evidence of good feeling, bringing to us of their food, signaling to us where for the safety of the ship we ought to anchor in the port, continually accompanying us until we cast anchor there.

In which we remained XV days, supplying ourselves with many necessities; where every day the people came to see us at the ship, bringing their women, of whom they are very careful; because, entering the ship themselves, remaining a long time, they made their women stay in the barges, and however many entreaties we made them, offering to give them various things, it was not possible that they would allow them to enter the ship. And one of the two Kings coming many times with the Queen and many attendants through their desire to see us, at first always stopt on a land distant from us two hundred paces, sending a boat to inform us of their coming, saying they wished to come to see the ship; doing this for a kind of safety.

And when they had the response from us, they came quickly, and having stood awhile to look, hearing the noisy clamor of the sailor crowd, sent the Queen with her damsels in a very light barge to stay on a little island distant from us a quarter of a league; himself remaining a very long time, discoursing by signs and gestures of various fanciful ideas, examining all the equipments of the ship, asking especially their purpose, imitating our manners, tasting our foods, then parted from us benignantly. And one time, our people remaining two or three days on a little island near the ship for various necessities as is the custom of sailors, he came with seven or eight of his attendants, watching our operations, asking many times if we wished to remain there for a long time, offering us his every help. Then, shooting with the bow, running, he performed with his attendants various games to give us pleasure.

Many times we were from five to six leagues inland, which we found as pleasing as it can be to narrate, adapted to every kind of cultivation—grain, wine, oil. Because in that place the fields are from XXV to XXX leagues wide, open and devoid of every impediment of trees, of such fertility that any seed in them would produce the best crops. Entering then into the woods, all of which are penetrable by any numerous army in any way whatsoever, and whose trees, oaks, cypresses, and others are unknown in our Europe. We found Lucallian apples, plums, and filberts, and many kinds of fruits different from ours. Animals there are in very great number, stags, deer, lynx, and other species, which, in the way of the others, they capture with snares and bows, which are their principal arms. The arrows of whom are worked with great beauty, placing at the end, instead of iron, emery, jasper, hard marble, and other sharp stones, by which they served themselves instead of iron in cutting trees, making their barges from a single trunk of a tree, hollowed with wonderful skill, in which from fourteen to XV men will go comfortably; the short oar, broad at the end, working it solely with the strength of the arms at sea without any peril, with as much speed as pleases them.

Going further, we saw their habitations, circular in form, of XIIII to XV paces compass, made from semi-circles of wood [*i.e.*, arched saplings, bent in the form of an arbor], separated one from the other, without system of architecture, covered with mats of straw ingeniously worked, which protect them from rain and wind. There is no doubt that if they had the perfection of the arts we have, they would build magnificent edifices, for all the maritime coast is full of blue rocks, crystals and alabaster; and for such cause is full of ports and shelters for ships. They change said houses from one place to another according to the opulence of the site and the season in which they live. Carrying away only the mats, immediately they have other habitations made. There live in each a father and family to a very large number, so that in some we saw XXV and XXX souls. Their food is like the others: of pulse (which they produce with more system of culture than the others, observing the full moon, the rising of the Pleiades, and many customs derived from the ancients), also of the chase and fish. They live a long time and rarely incur illness; if they are opprest with wounds, without crying they cure themselves by themselves with fire, their end being of old age. We judge they are very compassionate and charitable toward their relatives, making them great lamentations in their adversities, in their grief calling to mind all their good fortunes. The relatives, one with another, at the end of their life use the Sicilian lamentation, mingled with singing lasting a long time. This is as much as we were able to learn about them.

The land is situated in the parallel of Rome, in forty and two-thirds degrees, but somewhat colder on account of chance and not on account of nature, as I will narrate to Your Majesty in another part, describing at present the situation of said port. The shore of said land runs from west to east. The mouth of the port looks toward the south, half a league wide, after entering which between east and north it extends XII leagues, where, widening itself, it makes an ample bay of about XX leagues in circuit. In which are five little islands of much fertility and beauty, full of high and spreading trees, among which any numerous fleet, without fear of tempest or other impediment of fortune, could rest securely. Turning thence toward the south to the entrance of the port, on one side and the other are very charming hills with many brooks, which from the height to the sea discharge clear waters, which on account of its beauty we called "Refugio."

In the midst of the mouth is found a rock of Petra Viva produced by nature, adapted for the building of any desired engine or bulwark for its protection, which on account of the nature of the stone and on account of the family of a gentlewoman we called "La Petra Viva"; on whose right side at said mouth of the port is a promontory which we called "Jovio Promontory."

Being supplied with our every necessity, the 6th day of May we departed from said port, following the shore, never losing sight of the land. We sailed one hundred and fifty leagues, within which space we found shoals which extend from the continent into the sea 50 leagues. Upon which there was over three feet of water; on account of which great danger in navigating it, we survived with difficulty and baptized it "Armellini," finding it of the same nature and somewhat higher with some mountains, with a high promontory which we named "Pallavisino," [7] which all indicated minerals. We did not stop there because the favorableness of the weather served us in sailing along the coast: we think it must conform to the other. The shore ran to the east.

In the space of fifty leagues, holding more to the north, we found a high land full of very thick forests, the trees of which were pines, cypresses and such as grow in cold regions. The people all different from the others, and as much as those passed were of cultivated manners, these were full of uncouthness and vices, so barbarous that we were never able, with howsoever many signs we made them, to have any intercourse with them. They dress with the skins of bear, lynxes, sea-wolves, and other animals. The food, according to that which we were able to learn through going many times to their habitations, we think is of the chase, fish, and some products which are of a species of roots which the ground yields by its own self. They do not have pulse, nor did we see any signs of cultivation, nor would the ground, on account of its sterility, be adapted to produce fruit or any grain. If, trading at any time with them, we desired their things, they came to the shore of the sea upon some rock where it was very steep, and—we remaining in the small boat—with a cord let down to us what they wished to give, continually crying on land that we should not approach, giving quickly the barter, not taking in exchange for it except knives, hooks for fishing, and sharp metal. They had no regard for courtesy, and when they had nothing more to exchange, at their departing the men made at us all the signs of contempt and shame which any brute creature could make. Contrary to their wish, XXV armed men of us were inland two and three leagues, and when we descended to the shore they shot at us with their bows, sending forth the greatest cries, then fled into the woods. We do not know any value of any moment in this land, except the very great forests, with some hills which possibly have some metal, because on many [natives] we saw "paternosters" of copper in the ears.

We departed, skirting the coast between east and north, which we found very beautiful, open and bare of forests, with high mountains back inland, growing smaller toward the shore of the sea. In fifty leagues we discovered XXXII islands, among which we called the three larger "The Three Daughters of Navarra," all near to the continent, small and of pleasing appearance, high, following the curving of the land, among which were formed most beautiful ports and channels, as are formed in the Adriatic Gulf, in the Illyrias, and Dalmatia. We had no intercourse with the peoples and think they were, like the others, devoid of morals and culture.

Navigating between east-southeast and north-northeast, in the space of CL leagues, we came near the land which the Britons found in the past, by the Cabots, [8] which stands in fifty degrees, and having consumed all our naval stores and victuals, having discovered six hundred leagues and more of new land, furnishing ourselves with water and wood, we decided to turn toward France.

CARTIER'S EXPLORATION OF THE ST. LAWRENCE (1534)

I-THE ACCOUNT GIVEN BY JOHN A. DOYLE [1]

Jacques Cartier was a brave and experienced sea captain from St. Malo. In 1534, Cartier made a preliminary voyage of exploration. Touching at Newfoundland, he sailed through the straits of Belle Isle and explored the east shore of the island, a region which for the barrenness of its soil and the severity of its climate seemed the very spot whither Cain had been banished. The coast of New Brunswick held out a more inviting prospect. The fertility of the soil reminded the voyagers of their native Brittany, and one field there seemed worth more than the whole of Newfoundland. Thence Cartier sailed into the Gulf of St. Lawrence, and would have explored the great river of Canada, but storms arose and he deemed it prudent to return to France before bad weather set in. His report of the country was encouraging. The soil, as we have seen, promised well, and the voyagers had not yet learned the terrors of a Canadian winter. The natives were rude in their habits, but they were uniformly peaceful and ready to trade on easy terms for such goods as they possest. There seemed good reason to hope, too, that they might be converted to Christianity, and one of them had shown confidence enough in the strangers to trust them with his two children, who were easily reconciled to their captivity by the gift of red caps and colored shirts.

In the next year Cartier again went forth with three ships. After confessing and taking the sacrament in the church of St. Malo, the adventurers set sail on Whit Sunday. Among them was the cup-bearer to the Dauphin, Claudius de Pont-Briand. As before, the strangers were well received by the Indians, and landed safely at Quebec. There Cartier left his sailors with instructions to make a fortified camp, while he himself, with the greater part of his men-at-arms and his two Indian captives of the year before, should explore the upper banks of the St. Lawrence, and penetrate, if possible, to the great Indian city of Hochelaga. [2] The Indians, tho outwardly friendly, seem either to have distrusted the French, or else grudged their neighbors at Hochelaga such valuable allies, and would have dissuaded Cartier from his expedition. When their remonstrances proved useless, the savages tried to work on the fears of the visitors. Three canoes came floating down the river, each containing a fiendish figure with horns and blackened face. The supposed demons delivered themselves of a threatening harangue, and then paddled to the shore, and whether to complete the performance, or through honest terror, fell fainting in their boats. The Indians then explained to Cartier that their god had sent a warning to the presumptuous strangers, bidding them refrain from the intended voyage. Cartier replied that the Indian god could have no power over those who believed in Christ. The Indians acquiesced, and even affected to rejoice in the approaching discomfiture of their deity. Cartier and his followers started on the voyage.

After a fortnight's journey they came in sight of the natural citadel of Hochelaga, the royal mount, as they fitly called it, which has since given its name to the stately city below. The site of that city was then filled by a village surrounded by maize fields and strongly fortified after the Iroquois manner. There the French were received with hospitality and with a reverence which seemed to imply that they were something more than mortal. The sick were laid before them to be healed, and when Cartier read portions of the Gospel in French, the savages listened reverently to the unknown sounds. On his return, Cartier found his fort securely palisaded, and decided there to await the winter. So far all had gone well, but the settlers were soon destined to see the unfavorable side of Canadian life. The savages, after their fickle nature, began to waver in their friendship. A worse danger was to come. Scurvy broke out, and before long twenty-five men had died, and not more than three or four remained well. At length the leaf of a tree whose virtues were pointed out by the Indians restored the sufferers to health. When winter disappeared and the river again became navigable, Cartier determined to return. He was anxious that the French king should learn the wonders of the country from the mouths of its own people. Accordingly, with a characteristic mixture of caution, subtlety, and conciliation, he allured the principal chief Donnacona, and some of his followers into the fort. There they were seized and carried to the ships, nominally as honored guests, like Montezuma among the followers of Cortez. Cartier then set sail with his captives, and in July reached St. Malo. The Indians, as was usually the fate of such captives, pined under a strange sky, and when Cartier sailed again not one was alive.

Four years elapsed before another voyage was undertaken. In 1540 a fleet of five ships was made ready at the expense of the king, who reserved to himself a third of the profits of the voyage. Cartier was appointed captain-general, with instructions to establish a settlement and to labor for the conversion of the savages. With Cartier was associated a man of high birth, the Sieur de Roberval, who was appointed Viceroy and Lieutenant-general of Newfoundland, Labrador, and all the territory explored by Cartier, with the title of Lord of Norumbega. This division of command seems to have led to no good results. Another measure which probably contributed to the failure of the expedition was the mode employed for raising the necessary crews. Cartier, like Frobisher, was empowered to search the prisons for recruits. Even before the voyage began things took an unfavorable turn. Roberval's ammunition was not ready at the stated time, and the departure of the fleet was thereby hindered.

At length, lest further delay should give offense at court, Cartier sailed, leaving Roberval to follow. The first interview with the savages was a source of some fear, as it was doubtful how they would receive the tidings of Donnacona's death. Luckily, the chief to whom the news was first told was Donnacona's successor, and, as might have been expected, he showed no dissatisfaction at Cartier's story. The French then settled themselves in their old quarters at Quebec. Two of the four ships were sent home to France to report safe arrival of the expedition, while Cartier himself, with two boats, set out to explore the river above Hochelaga. After his departure the relations between the settlers and the Indians became unfriendly, a change probably due in part to the loss of Donnacona and his companions. Whatever the cause, the danger seemed so serious that Cartier on his return decided to abandon the colony and to make for France. From later events it would seem as if Cartier had no friendly feeling toward Roberval, and jealousy may have had some share in leading him to forsake the enterprise for which he had endured and risked so much. On his homeward voyage he put into the harbor of St. John, in Newfoundland. There he met Roberval with three ships and 200 men. Their meeting seems to have been friendly, but Cartier, instead of obeying Roberval's orders and returning with him to Canada, quietly weighed anchor in the night and sailed away to France.

With this inglorious departure ends the career of the first great French colonizer. Robervai resumed his voyage and landed above Quebec. There he built a single abode for the whole colony on the model of a college or monastery, with a common hail and kitchen. Of the doings of the settlers we have but scanty accounts, but we learn enough to see that the colony was ill-planned from the outset, and that either Roberval was unfit for command or singularly unfortunate in his subjects. The supplies were soon found to be inadequate, and scurvy set in, the colonists became disorderly, and Roberval ruled them with a rod of iron. Trifling offenses were punished with fearful severity; men and women were flogged, and if we may believe one account, the punishment of death was inflicted with no sparing hand. How long the colony lingered on is unknown. Roberval himself returned to France only, it is said, to die a violent death in the streets of Paris. There is nothing to tell us whether his colonists returned with him or whether, like White's unhappy followers, they were left to fall victims to the horrors of the wilderness. Whatever was their fate, no attempt was made to restore the colony, and the St. Lawrence was left for more than fifty years to the savages and wild beasts.

II-CARTIER'S OWN ACCOUNT [1]

Vpon Thursday being the eight of the moneth, because the winde was not good to go out with our ships, we set our boates in a readinesse to goe to discouer the said Bay [2] , and that day wee went 25 leagues within it. The next day the wind and weather being faire, we sailed vntil noone, in which time we had notice of a great part of the said Bay, and how that ouer the low lands, there were other lands with high mountaines: but seeing that there was no passage at all, wee began to turne back againe, taking our way along the coast and sayling, we saw certaine wilde men.... and by and by in clusters they came to the shore where we were, with their boates, bringing with them skinnes and other such things as they had, to haue of our wares.... til they had nothing but their naked bodies; for they gaue vs all whatsoeuer they had, and that was but of small value. We perceiued that this people might very easily be conuerted to our Religion. They goe from place to place. They liue onely with fishing. They haue an ordinarie time to fish for their prouision. The countrey is hotter than the countrey of Spaine, and the fairest that can possibly be found, altogether smooth, and leuel. There is no place be it neuer so little, but it bath some trees (yea albeit it be sandie) or else is full of wilde corne, that hath an eare like vnto Rie: the corne is like oates, and smal peason as thicke as if they had bene sowen and plowed, white and red Roses, with many other flouers of very sweet and pleasant smell. There be also many goodly medowes full of grasse, and lakes wherein great plentie of salmons be. They call a hatchet in their tongue Cochi, and a knife Bacon: we named it The bay of heat....

The Saturday following, being the first of August, by Sunne rising, wee had certaine other landes, lying North and Northeast, that were very high and craggie, and seemed to be mountaines: betweene which were other low lands with woods and riuers: wee went about the sayd lands, as well on the one side as on the other, still bending Northwest, to see if it were either a gulfe, or a passage, vntill the fift of the moneth. The distance from one land to the other is about fifteene leagues. The middle between them both is 50 degrees and a terce in latitude. We had much adoe to go fiue miles farther, the winds were so great and the tide against vs. And at fiue miles end, we might plainely see and perceiue land on both sides, which there beginneth to spread it selfe.

After we had sailed along the sayd coast, for the space of two houres, behold, the tide began to tame against vs, with so swift and raging a course, that it was not possible for vs with 13 oares to row or get one stones cast farther, so that we were constrained to leaue our boates with some of our men to guard them, and 10 or 12 men went ashore to the sayd Cape, where we found that the land beginneth to bend Southwest, which hauing scene, we came to our boats againe, and so to our ships, which were stil ready vnder salle, hoping to go forward; but for all that, they were fallen more then four leagues to leeward from the place where we had left them, where so soone as we came, wee assembled together all our Captaines, Masters, and Mariners, to haue their aduice and opinion what was best to be done; and after that euery one had said, considering that the Easterly winds began to beare away, and blow, and that the flood was so great, that we did but fall, and that there was nothing to be gotten, and that stormes and tempests began to reigne in Newfoundland, and that we were so farre from home, not knowing the perils and dangers that were behind, for either we must agree to reture home againe, or els to stay there all the yeere. More ouer, we did consider, that if the Northerne winds did take vs, it were not possible for vs to depart thence. All which opinions being heard and considered, we altogether determined to addresse our selues homeward. Nowe because vpon Saint Peters day wee entred into the sayd Streite, we named it Saint Peters Streite....

In the yeere of our Lord 1535, vpon Whitsunday, being the 16. of May, by the commandement of our Captaine Iames Cartier, and with a common accord, in the Cathedrall Church of S. Malo we deuoutly each one confessed our selues, and receiued the Sacrament: and all entring into the Quier of the sayd Church, wee presented our selues before the Reuerend Father in Christ, the Lord Bishop of S. Malo, who blessed vs all, being in his Bishops roabes. The Wednesday following, being the 19. of May, there arose a good gale of wind, and therefore we hoysed seyle with three ships.... We staied and rested our selues in the sayd hauen, vntill the seuenth of August being Sonday: on which day we hoysed sayle, and came toward land on the South side toward Cape Robast, distant from the sayd hauen about twentie leagues Northnortheast, and Southsouthwest: but the next day there rose a stormie and a contrary winde, and because we could find no hauen there toward the South, thence we went coasting along toward the North, beyond the abouesayd hauen about ten leagues, where we found a goodly great gulfe, full of Islands, passages, and entrances, toward what wind soeuer you please to bend: for the knowledge of this gulfe there is a great Island that is like to a Cape of lande, stretching somewhat further foorth than the others, and about two leagues within the land, there is an hill fashioned as it were an heape of corne. We named the sayd gulfe Saint Laurence his bay. The twelfth of the sayd moneth wee went from the sayd Saint Laurence his Bay, or gulfe, sayling Westward, and discouered a Cape of land toward the South, that runneth West and by South, distant from the sayd Saint Laurence his Bay, about fiue and twenty leagues....

Moreouer, I beleeue that there were neuer so many Whales seen as we saw that day about the sayd Cape. The next day after being aur Ladie day of August the fifteenth of the moneth, hauing passed the Straight, we had notice of certaine lands that wee left toward the South, which landes are full of uery great and high hilles, and this Cape wee named The Island of the Assumption, and perceuived to be higher than the Southerly, more then thirty leagues in length. We treaded the sayd landes about toward the South: from the sayd day vntill Tewesday noone following, the winde came West, and therefore wee bended toward the North, purposing to goe and see the land that we before had spied. Being arriued there, we found the sayd landes as it were ioyned together, and low toward the Sea. And the Northerly mountaines that are vpon the sayd low lands stretch East, and West, and a quarter of the South. Our wild men told vs that there was the beginning of Saguenay, and that it was land inhabited, and that thence commeth the red Copper, of them named Caignetdaze.

There is between the Southerly lands, and the Northerly about thirty leagues distance, and more then two hundredth fadome depth. The sayd men did moreouer certifie vnto vs, that there was the way and beginning of the great riuer of Hochelaga and ready way to Canada, which riuer the further it went the narrower it came, euen vnto Canada, and that then there was fresh water, which went so famine vpwards, that they had neuer heard of any man who had gone to the head of it, and that there is no other passage but with small boates.... Vpon the first of September we departed out of the said hauen, purposing to go toward Canada; and about 15 leagues from it toward the West, and Westsouthwest, amidst the riuer, there are three Islands, ouer against the which there is a riuer which runneth swift, and is of great depth, and it is that which leadeth, and runneth into the countrey and kingdome of Saguenay, as by the two wild men of Canada it was told vs. This riuer passeth and runneth along very high and steepe hills of bare stone, where uery little earth is, and notwithstanding there is a great quantity of sundry sorts of trees that grow in the said bare stones, euen as vpon good and fertile ground, in such sort that we haue seene some so great as wel would suffise to make a mast for a ship of 30 tunne burden, and as greene as possibly can be, growing in a stony rocke without any earth at all....

The seuenth of the moneth being our Ladies euen, after seruice we went from that Iland to go vp higher into the riuer, and came to 14 Ilands seuen or eight leagues from the Iland of Filberds, where the countrey of Canada beginneth, one of which Ilands is ten leagues in length, and fiue in bredth, greatly inhabited of such men as onely liue by fishing of such sorts of fishes as the riuer affordeth, according to the season of them.... The next day following, the Lord of Canada (whose proper name was Donnacona, but by the name of Lord they call him Agouhanna) with twelue boats came to our ships, accompanied with many people, who causing ten of his boates to goe backe with the other two, approched vnto vs with sixteene men ... Our Captaine then caused our boates to be set in order, that with the next tide he might goe vp higher into the riuer, to find some safe harborough for our ships: and we passed vp the riuer against the streame about tenne leagues, coasting the said Iland, at the end whereof, we found a goodly and pleasant sound, where is a little riuer and hauen, where by reason of the flood there is about three fadome water. This place seemed to us very fit and commodious to harbour our ships therein, and so we did very safely, we named it the holy Crosse, for on that day we came thither. Neere vnto it, there is a village, whereof Donnacona is Lord, and there he keepeth his abode: it is called Stadacona [Quebec] as goodly a plot of ground as possibly may be seene.

Hauing considered the place, and finding it fit for our purpose, our Captaine withdrew himselfe on purpose to returne to our ships. After we were come with our boats vnto our ships againe, our Captaine cause our barks to be made readie to goe on land in the said Iland, to note the trees that in shew seemed so faire, and to consider the nature and qualitie of it: which things we did, and found it full of goodly trees like to ours. Also we saw many goodly Vines, a thing not before of vs seene in those countries, and therefore we named it Bacchus Iland. It is in length about twelue leagues, in sight very pleasant, but full of woods, no part of it manured, vnless it be in certaine places, where a few cottages be for Fishers dwellings as before we haue said....

The next day being the 19 of September we hoysed saile, and with our Pinnesse and two boates departed to goe vp the riuer with the flood, where on both shores of it we beganne to see as goodly a countrey as possibly can with eye seene, all replenished with very goodly trees, and Vines laden as full of grapes as could be all along the riuer, which rather seemed to haue bin planted by mans hand than otherwise. True it is, that because they are not dressed and wrought as they should be, their bunches of grapes are not so great nor sweete as ours.... From the nineteenth vntill the eight and twentieth of September, we sailed vp along the saide riuer, neuer losing one houre of time, all which time we saw as goodly and pleasant a countrey as possibly can be wished for....

The next day our Captaine seeing for that time it was not possible for our Pinesse to goe on any further, he caused our boates to be made readie, and as much munition and victuals to be put in them, as they could well beare: he departed with them, accompanyed with many Gentlemen, that is to say, Claudius of Ponte Briand, Cupbearer to the Lorde Dolphin of France, Charles of Pommeraye, Iohn Gouion, Iohn Powlet, with twentie and eight Mariners: and Mace Iallobert, and William Briton, who had the charge vnder the Captaine of the other two ships, to goe vp as farre as they could into that riuer: we sayled with good and prosperous weather vntill the second of October, on which day we came to the towne of Hochelaga, [Montreal] distant from the place where we had left our Pinnesse fiue and fortie leagues.

SEARCHES FOR "THE SEVEN CITIES OF CIBOLA" (1530-1540)

THE ACCOUNT BY REUBEN GOLD THWAITES [1]

In 1513, a hundred and seven years before the landing of the Pilgrims at Plymouth, Balboa scaled the continental backbone at Darien and unfurled the flag of Spain by the waters of the Pacific. With wondrous zeal did Spanish explorers beat up and down the western shore of the Gulf of Mexico, seeking for an opening through. Cortez had no sooner secured possession of Mexico, after his frightful slaughter of the Aztecs, than he began pushing out to the west and northwest—along the "upper coasts of the South Sea"—in search of the strait which Montezuma told him existed.

It is unlikely that Montezuma's knowledge of North American geography was much greater than that of his conqueror. But in every age and land aborigines have first ascertained what visiting strangers most sought, whether it be gold or waterways, and assured them that somewhere beyond the neighboring horizon these objects were to be found in plenty. Spanish, French, and English have each in their turn chased American rainbows that existed only in the brains of imaginative tribesmen who had little other thought than a childish desire to gratify their guests.

Cortez undertook, at his own charge, several of these expensive exploring expeditions to discover the strait of which Montezuma had spoken, and one of them he conducted in person. In 1528—the year he visited Spain to meet his accusers—we find him dispatching Maldonado northward along the Pacific coast for three hundred miles; and five years later Grijalva and Jimenez were claiming for Spain the southern portion of Lower California. A full hundred years before Jean Nicolet related to the French authorities at their feeble outpost on the rock of Quebec the story of his daring progress into the wilds of the upper Mississippi Valley, and the rumors he had there heard of the great river which flowed into the South Sea, Spanish officials in the halls of Montezuma were receiving the tales of their adventurers, who had penetrated to strange lands laved by the waters of this selfsame ocean.

It was about the year 1530 when the Spaniards in Mexico first received word, through an itinerant monk, Marcos de Niza, of certain powerful semi-civilized tribes dwelling some six hundred miles north of the capital of the Aztecs. These strange people were said to possess in great store domestic utensils and ornaments made of gold and silver; to be massed in seven large cities composed of houses built with stone; and to be proficient in many of the arts of the Europeans. The search for "the seven cities of Cibola," as these reputed communities came to be called by the Spaniards, was at once begun.

Guzman, just then at the head of affairs in New Spain, zealously set forth at the head of four hundred Spanish soldiers, and a large following of Indians, to search for this marvelous country. But the farther north the army marched the more distant became Cibola in the report of the natives whom they met on the way; until at last the invaders became involved in the pathless deserts of New Mexico and the intricate ravines of the foothills beyond. The soldiers grew mutinous, and Guzman returned, crestfallen, to Mexico.

In April, 1528, three hundred enthusiastic young nobles and gentlemen from Spain landed at Tampa Bay, under the leadership of Narvaez, whom Cortez supplanted in the conquest of Mexico. Narvaez had been given a commission to hold Florida, with its supposed wealth of mines and precious stones, and to become its governor. Led by the customary fables of the natives, who told only such tales as they supposed their Spanish tormentors wished most to hear, the brilliant company wandered hither and thither through the vast swamps and forests, wasted by fatigue, famine, disease, and frequent assaults of savages. At last, after many distressing adventures, but four men were left—Cabeza de Vaca, treasurer of the expedition, and three others. For eight long years did these bruised and ragged Spaniards wearily roam across the region now divided into Texas, Indian Territory, Oklahoma, New Mexico, and Arizona—through tangled forests, across broad rivers, morasses, and desert stretches beset by wild beasts and men; but ever spurred on by vague reports of a colony of their countrymen to the southwest. At last (May, 1536), the miserable wanderers, first to make the transcontinental trip in northern latitudes, reached the Gulf of California, where they met some of their fellow countrymen, who bore them in triumph to the City of Mexico, as the guests of the province....

In that golden age of romance travelers were expected to gild their tales, and in this respect seldom failed to meet the popular demand. The Spanish conquistadores, in particular, lived in an atmosphere of fancy. They looked at American savages and their ways through Spanish spectacles; and knowing nothing of the modern science of ethnology, quite misunderstood the import of what they saw. Beset by the national vice of flowery embellishment, they were also pardonably ignorant of savage life, and had an indiscriminating thirst for the marvelous. Thus, we see plainly how the Cibola myth arose and grew; and why most official Spanish reports of the conquest of the Aztecs were so distorted by false conceptions of the conquered people as in some particulars to be of light value as material for history. It was, then, small wonder that Cabeza de Vaca and his fellow adventurers, in the midst of the hero worship of which they were now recipients, should claim themselves to have seen the mysterious seven cities, and to have enlarged upon the previous stories.

Coronado, governor of the northern province of New Galicia, was accordingly sent to conquer this wonderful country, which the adventurers had seen, but Guzman failed to find. In 1540, the years when Cortez again returned to meet ungrateful neglect at the bands of the Spanish court, Coronado set out with a well—equipped following of three hundred whites and eight hundred Indians. The Cibola cities were found to be but mud pueblos in Arizona and New Mexico, with the aspect of which we are to—day familiar; while the mild—tempered inhabitants, destitute of wealth, peacefully practising their crude industries and tilling their irrigated field, were foemen hardly worthy of Castilian steel.

CABEZA DE VACA'S JOURNEY TO THE SOUTHWEST (1535-1536)

DE VACA'S OWN ACCOUNT [1]

Castillo returned at the end of three days to the spot where he had left us, and brought five or six of the people. He told us he had found fixt dwellings of civilization, that the inhabitants lived on beans and pumpkins, and that he had seen maize. This news the most of anything delighted us, and for it we gave infinite thanks to our Lord. Castillo told us the negro was coming with all the population to wait for us in the road not far off. Accordingly we left, and, having traveled a league and a half, we met the negro and the people coming to receive us. They gave us beans, many pumpkins, calabashes, blankets of cowhide and other things. As this people and those who came with us were enemies, and spoke not each other's language, we discharged the latter, giving them what we received, and departed with the others. Six leagues from there, as the night set in, we arrived at the houses, where great festivities were made over us. We remained one day, and the next set out with these Indians. They took us to the settled habitations of others, who lived upon the same food. From that place onward was another usage. Those who knew of our approach did not come out to receive us on the road as the others had done, but we found them in their houses, and they had made others for our reception. They were all seated with their faces turned to the wall, their heads down, the hair brought before their eyes, and their property placed in a heap in the middle of the house. From this place they began to give us many blankets of skin; and they had nothing they did not bestow. They have the finest persons of any people we saw, of the greatest activity and strength, who best understood us and intelligently answered our inquiries. We called them the Cow nation, because most of the cattle [2] killed are slaughtered in their neighborhood, and along up that river for over fifty leagues they destroy great numbers.

They go entirely naked after the manner of the first we saw. The women are drest with deer skin, and some few men, mostly the aged, who are incapable of fighting. The country is very populous. We asked how it was they did not plant maize. They answered it was that they might not lose what they should put in the ground; that the rains had failed for two years in succession, and the seasons were so dry the seed had everywhere been taken by the moles, and they could not venture to plant again until after water had fallen copiously. They begged us to tell the sky to rain, and to pray for it, and we said we would do so. We also desired to know whence they got the maize, and they told us from where the sun goes down; there it grew throughout the region, and the nearest was by that path....

Two days being spent while we tarried, we resolved to go in search of the maize. We did not wish to follow the path leading to where the cattle are, because it is toward the north, and for us very circuitous, since we ever held it certain that going toward the sunset we must find what we desired.

Thus we took our way, and traversed all the country until coming out at the South Sea. Nor was the dread we had of the sharp hunger through which we should have to pass (as in verity we did, throughout the seventeen days' journey of which the natives spoke) sufficient to hinder us. During all that time, in ascending by the river, they gave us many coverings of cowhide; but we did not eat of the fruit. Our sustenance each day was about a handful of deer-suet, which we had a long time been used to saving for such trials. Thus we passed the entire journey of seventeen days.

As the sun went down, upon some plains that lie between chains of very great mountains, we found a people who for the third part of the year eat nothing but the powder of straw, and, that being the season when we passed, we also had to eat of it, until reaching permanent habitations, where was abundance of maize brought together. They gave us a large quantity in grain and flour, pumpkins, beans, and shawls of cotton. With all these we loaded our guides, who went back the happiest creatures on earth. We gave thanks to God, our Lord, for having brought us where we had found so much food.

Some houses are of earth, the rest all of cane mats. From this point we marched through more than a hundred leagues of country, and continually found settled domicils, with plenty of maize and beans. The people gave us many deer and cotton shawls better than those of New Spain, many beads and certain corals found on the South Sea, and fine turquoises that come from the North. Indeed, they gave us everything they had. To me they gave five emeralds made into arrow heads, which they use at their singing and dancing. They appeared to be very precious. I asked whence they got these; and they said the stones were brought from some lofty mountains that stand toward the north, where were populous towns and very large houses, and that they were purchased with plumes and the feathers of parrots.

Among this people the women are treated with more decorum than in any part of the Indias we had visited. They wear a shirt of cotton that falls as low as the knee, and over it half sleeves with skirts reaching to the ground, made of drest deerskin. It opens in front, and is brought close with straps of leather. They soap this with a certain root that cleanses well, by which they are enabled to keep it becomingly. Shoes are worn. The people all came to us that we should touch and bless them, they being very urgent, which we could accomplish only with great labor, for sick and well all wished to go with a benediction.

These Indians ever accompanied us until they delivered us to others; and all held full faith in our coming from heaven. While traveling, we went without food all day until night, and we ate so little as to astonish them. We never felt exhaustion, neither were we in fact at all weary, so inured were we to hardship. We possest great influence and authority: to preserve both, we seldom talked with them. The negro was in constant conversation; he informed himself about the ways we wished to take, of the towns there were, and the matters we desired to know.

We passed through many and dissimilar tongues. Our Lord granted us favor with the people who spoke them, for they always understood us, and we them. We questioned them, and received their answers by signs, just as if they spoke our language and we theirs; for, altho we knew six languages, we could not everywhere avail ourselves of them, there being a thousand differences.

Throughout all these countries the people who were at war immediately made friends, that they might come to meet us, and bring what they possest. In this way we left all the land at peace, and we taught all the inhabitants by signs, which they understood, that in heaven was a Man we called God, who had created the sky and earth; Him we worshiped and had for our Master; that we did what He commanded, and from His hand came all good; and would they do as we did, all would be well with them. So ready of apprehension we found them that, could we have have the use of language by which to make ourselves perfectly understood, we should have left them all Christians. Thus much we gave them to understand the best we could. And afterward, when the sun rose, they opened their hands together with loud shouting toward the heavens, and then drew them down all over their bodies. They did the same again when the sun went down. They are a people of good condition and substance, capable in any pursuit. In the town where the emeralds were presented to us the people gave Dorantes over six hundred open hearts of deer. They ever keep a good supply of them for food, and we called the place Pueblo de los Corazones. It is the entrance into many provinces on the South Sea. They who go to look for them, and do not enter there, will be lost. On the coast is no maize: the inhabitants eat the powder of rush and of straw, and fish that is caught in the sea from rafts, not having canoes. With grass and straw the women cover their nudity. They are a timid and dejected people.

We think that near the coast by way of those towns through which we came are more than a thousand leagues of inhabited country, plentiful of subsistence. Three times the year it is planted with maize and beans. Deer are of three kinds; one the size of the young steer of Spain. There are innumerable houses, such as are called bahios. They have poison from a certain tree the size of the apple. For effect no more is necessary than to pluck the fruit and moisten the arrow with it, or, if there be no fruit, to break a twig and with the milk do the like. The tree is abundant, and so deadly that, if the leaves be bruised and steeped in some neighboring water, the deer and other animals drinking it soon burst.

We were in this town three days. A day's journey farther was another town, at which the rain fell heavily while we were there, and the river became so swollen we could not cross it, which detained us fifteen days. In this time Castillo saw the buckle of a sword-belt on the neck of an Indian, and stitched to it the nail of a horseshoe. He took them, and we asked the native what they were: he answered that they came from heaven. We questioned him further, as to who had brought them thence: they all responded that certain men who wore beards like us had come from heaven and arrived at that river, bringing horses, lances, and swords, and that they had lanced two Indians. In a manner of the utmost indifference we could feign, we asked them what had become of those men. They answered that they had gone to sea, putting their lances beneath the water, and going themselves also under the water: afterward that they were seen on the surface going toward the sunset. For this we gave many thanks to God our Lord. We had before despaired of ever hearing more of Christians. Even yet we were left in great doubt and anxiety, thinking those people were merely persons who had come by sea on discoveries. However, as we had now such exact information, we made greater speed, and, as we advanced on our way, the news of the Christians continually grew. We told the natives that we were going in search of that people, to order them not to kill nor make slaves of them, nor take them from their lands, nor do other injustice. Of this the Indians were very glad.

We passed through many territories and found them all vacant; their inhabitants wandered fleeing among the mountains, without daring to have houses or till the earth for fear of Christians. The sight was one of infinite pain to us, a land very fertile and beautiful, abounding in springs and streams, the hamlets deserted and burned, the people thin and weak, all fleeing or in concealment. As they did not plant, they appeased their keen hunger by eating roots and the bark of trees. We bore a share in the famine along the whole way; for poorly could these unfortunates provide for us, themselves being so reduced they looked as tho they would willingly die. They brought shawls of those they had concealed because of the Christians presenting them to us; and they related how the Christians at other times had come through the land, destroying and burning the towns, carrying away half the men, and all the women and the boys, while those who had been able to escape were wandering about fugitives. We found them so alarmed they dared not remain anywhere. They would not nor could they till the earth, but preferred to die rather than live in dread of such cruel usage as they received. Altho these showed themselves greatly delighted with us, we feared that on our arrival among those who held the frontier, and fought against the Christians, they would treat us badly, and revenge upon us the conduct of their enemies; but, when God our Lord was pleased to bring us there, they began to dread and respect us as the others had done, and even somewhat more, at which we no little wondered. Thence it may at once be seen that, to bring all these people to be Christians and to the obedience of the Imperial Majesty, they must be won by kindness, which is a way certain, and no other is.

They took us to a town on the edge of a range of mountains, to which the ascent is over difficult crags. We found many people there collected out of fear of the Christians. They received us well, and presented us all they had. They gave us more than two thousand back-loads of maize, which we gave to the distrest and hungered beings who guided us to that place. The next day we dispatched four messengers through the country, as we were accustomed to do, that they should call together all the rest of the Indians at a town distant three days' march. We set out the day after with all the people. The tracks of the Christians and marks where they slept were continually seen. At mid-day we met our messengers, who told us they had found no Indians, that they were roving and hiding in the forests, fleeing that the Christians might not kill nor make them slaves; the night before they had observed the Christians from behind trees, and discovered what they were about, carrying away many people in chains....

From this spot, called the river Petutan, to the river to which Diego de Guzman came, where we heard of Christians, may be as many as eighty leagues; thence to the town where the rains overtook us, twelve leagues, and that is twelve leagues from the South Sea. Throughout this region, wheresoever the mountains extend, we saw clear traces of gold and lead, iron, copper, and other metals. Where the settled habitations are, the climate is hot; even in January the weather is very warm. Thence toward the meridian, the country unoccupied to the North Sea is unhappy and sterile. There we underwent great and incredible hunger. Those who inhabit and wander over it are a race of evil inclination and most cruel customs. The people of the fixt residences and those beyond regard silver and gold with indifference, nor can they conceive of any use for them.

When we saw sure signs of Christians, and heard how near we were to them, we gave thanks to God our Lord for having chosen to bring us out of a captivity so melancholy and wretched. The delight we felt let each one conjecture, when if he shall remember the length of time we were in that country, the suffering and perils we underwent. That night I entreated my companions that one of them should go back three days' journey after the Christians who were moving about over the country, where we had given assurance of protection. Neither of them received this proposal well, excusing themselves because of weariness and exhaustion; and altho either might have done better than I, being more youthful and athletic, yet seeing their unwillingness, the next morning I took the negro with eleven Indians, and, following the Christians by their trail, I traveled ten leagues, passing three villages, at which they had slept.

The day after I overtook four of them on horseback, who were astonished at the sight of me, so strangely habited as I was, and in company with Indians. They stood staring at me a length of time, so confounded that they neither hailed me nor drew near to make an inquiry. I bade them take me to their chief: accordingly we went together half a league to the place where was Diego de Alcaraz, their captain.

After we had conversed, he stated to me that he was completely undone; he had not been able in a long time to take any Indians; he knew not which way to turn, and his men had well begun to experience hunger and fatigue. I told him of Castillo and Dorantes, who were behind, ten leagues off, with a multitude that conducted us. He thereupon sent three cavalry to them, with fifty of the Indians who accompanied him. The negro returned to guide them, while I remained. I asked the Christians to give me a certificate of the year, month, and day I arrived there, and of the manner of my coming, which they accordingly did. From this river to the town of the Christians, named San Miguel, within the government of the province called New Galicia, are thirty leagues.

THE EXPEDITION OF CORONADO TO THE SOUTHWEST (1540-1541)

CORONADO'S OWN ACCOUNT [1]

At length I arriued at the valley of the people called Caracones, the 26. day of the moneth of May: and from Culiacan vntill I came thither, I could not helpe my selfe, saue onely with a great quantitie of bread of Maiz: for seeing the Maiz in the fieldes were not yet ripe, I was constrained to leaue them all behind me. In this valley of the Caracones wee found more store of people than in any other part of the Countrey which we had passed, and great store of tillage. But I understood that there was store thereof in another valley called The Lords valley, which I woulde not disturbe with force, but sent thither Melchior Diaz with wares of exchange to procure some, and to giue the sayde Maiz to the Indians our friendes which wee brought with vs, and to some others that had lost their cattell in the way, and were not able to carry their victuals so farre which they brought from Culiacan. It pleased God that wee gate some small quantitie of Maiz with this traffique, whereby certaine Indians were relieued and some Spanyards.

And by that time that wee were come to this valley of the Caracones, some tenne or twelue of our horses were dead through wearinesse: for being ouercharged with great burdens, and hauing but little meate, they could not endure the trauaile. Likewise some of our Negros and some of our Indians dyed here; which was no small want vnto vs for the performance of our enterprise. They tolde me that this valley of the Caracones is fiue days iourney from the Westerne Sea. I sent for the Indians of the Sea coast to vnderstand their estate, and while I stayed for them the horses rested: and I stayed there foure days, in which space the Indians of the Sea coast came vnto mee: which told mee, that two dayes sayling from their coast of the Sea, there were seuen or eight Islands right ouer against them, well inhabited with people, but badly furnished with victuals, and were a rude people: And they told mee, that they had seene a Shippe passe by not farre from the shore: which I wote not what to thinke whither it were one of those that went to discouer the Countrey, or else a Ship of the Portugals....

But after wee had passed these thirtie leagues, wee found fresh riuers, and grasse like that of Castile, and specially of that sort which we call Scaramoio, many Nutte trees and Mulberie trees, but the Nutte trees differ from those of Spayne in the leafe: and there was Flaxe, but chiefly neere the bankes of a certayne riuer which therefore wee called El Rio del Lino, that is say, the riuer of Flaxe: we found no Indians at all for a dayes trauaile, but afterward foure Indians came out vnto vs in peaceable maner, saying that they were sent euen to that desert place to signifie vnto vs that wee were welcome, and that the next day all the people would come out to meete vs on the way with victuals: and the master of the fielde gaue them a crosse, willing them to signifie to those of their citie that they should not feare, and they should rather let the people stay in their houses, because I came onely in the name of his Maiestie to defend and ayd them.

And this done, Fernando Aluardo returned to aduertise mee that certaine Indians were come vnto them in peaceable maner, and that two of them stayed for my comming with the master of the fielde. Whereupon I went vnto them and gaue them beades and certaine short slokes, willing them to returne vnto their citie, and bid them to stay quiet in their houses, and feare nothing. And this done I sent the master of the field to search whether there were any bad passage which the Indians might keepe against vs, and that hee should take and defend it vntill the next day that I shoulde come thither. So hee went, and found in the way a very bad passage, where wee might haue sustayned a very great harme: wherefore there hee seated himselfe with his company that were with him: and that very night the Indians came to take that passage to defend it, and finding it taken, they assaulted our men there, and as they tell mee, they assaulted them like valiant men; although in the ende they retired and fledde away; for the master of the fielde was watchfull, and was in order with his company: the Indians in token of retreate sounded on a certaine small trumpet, and did no hurt among the Spanyards. The very same night the master of the fielde certified mee hereof. Whereupon the next day in the best order that I could I departed in so great want of victuall, that I thought that if wee should stay one day longer without foode, wee should all perish for hunger, especially the Indians, for among vs all we had not two bushels of corne: wherefore it behooved mee to prike forward without delay. The Indians here and their made fires, and were answered againe afarre off as orderly as wee for our liues could haue done, to giue their fellowes vnderstanding, how wee marched and where we arriued....

As soone as I came within sight of this citie of Granada, I sent Don Garcias Lopez Campemaster, frier Daniel, and frier Luys, and Fernando Vermizzo somewhat before with certaine horsemen, to seeke the Indians and aduertise them that our comming was not to hurt them, but to defend them in the name of the Emperour our Lord, according as his maiestie had giuen vs in charge: which message was deliuered to the inhabitants of that countrey by an interpreter. But they like arrogant people made small account thereof; because we seemed very few in their eyes, and that they might destroy vs without any difficultie; and they strooke frier Luys with an arrow on the gowne, which by the grace of God did him no harme.

In the meane space I arriued with all the rest of the horsemen, and footemen, and found in the fleldes a great sort of the Indians which beganne to shoote at vs with their arrowes: and because I would obey your will and the commaund of the Marques, I woulde not let my people charge them, forbidding my company, which intreated mee that they might set vpon them, in any wise to prouoke them, saying that that which the enemies did was nothing, and that it was not meete to set vpon so fewe people. On the other side the Indians perceiuing that wee stirred not, tooke great stomacke and courage vnto them: insomuch that they came hard to our horses heeles to shoote at vs with their arrowes. Whereupon seeing that it was now time to stay no longer, and that the friers also were of the same opinion, I set vpon them without any danger: for suddenly they fled part to the citie which was neere and well fortified, and other into the field, which way they could shift: and some of the Indians were slaine, and more had beene if I would haue suffered them to haue bene pursued.

But considering that hereof we might reape but small profite, because the Indians that were without were fewe, and those which were retired into the cities, with them which stayed within at the first were many, where the victuals were whereof wee had so great neede, I assembled my people, and deuided them as I thought best to assault the citie, and I compassed it about: and because the famine which wee sustained suffered no delay, my selfe with certaine of these gentlemen and souldiers put our selues on foote, and commaunded that the crosse-bowes and harquebusiers shoulde giue the assault, and shoulde beate the enemies from the walles, that they might not hurt vs, and I assaulted the walles on one side, where they tolde me there was a scaling ladder set vp, and that there was one gate: but the crossebowmen suddenly brake the strings of their bowes, and the harquebusiers did nothing at all: for they came thither so weake and feeble, that scarcely they coulde stand on their feete.

And by this meanes the people that were aloft on the wals to defend the towne were no way hindered from doing vs all the mischiefe they could: so that twise they stroke mee to the ground with infinite number of great stones, which they cast downe: and if I had not beene defended with an excellent good headpiece which I ware, I thinke it had gone hardly with me: neuerthelesse my companie tooke mee vp with two small wounds in the face, and an arrowe sticking in my foote, and many blowes with stones on my armes and legges, and thus I went out of the battell very weake. I thinke that if Don Garcias Lopez de Cardenas the second time that they strooke mee to the ground had not succoured mee with striding ouer mee like a good knight, I had beene in farre greater danger then I was. But it pleased God that the Indians yeelded themselues vnto vs, and that this citie was taken: and such store of Maiz was found therein, as our necessitie required....

It remaineth now to certifie your Honour of the seuen cities, and of the kingdomes and prouinces whereof the Father prouinciall **[2]** made report vnto your Lordship. And to bee briefe, I can assure your honour, he sayd the trueth in nothing that he reported, but all was quite contrary, sauing onely the names of the cities, and great houses of stone: for although they bee not wrought with Turqueses, nor with lyme, nor brickes, yet are they very excellent good houses of three or foure or fiue lofts high, wherein are good lodgings and faire chambers with lathers instead of staires, and certaine cellars vnder the ground very good and paued, which are made for winter, they are in maner like stooues: and the lathers which they haue for their houses are all in a maner mooueable and portable, which are taken away and set downe when they please, and they are made of two pieces of wood with their steppes, as ours be. The seuen cities are seuen small townes, all made with these kinde of houses that I speake of: and they stand all within foure leagues together, and they are all called the kingdome of Cibola, and euery one of them haue their particular name: and none of them is called Cibola, but altogether they are called Cibola.

And this towne which I call a citie, I haue named Granada, as well because it is somewhat like vnto it, as also in remembrance of your lordship. In this towne where I nowe remaine, there may be some two hundred houses, all compassed with walles, and I thinke that with the rest of the houses which are not so walled, they may be together fiue hundred. There is another towne neere this, which is one of the seuen, & it is somwhat bigger than this, and another of the same bignesse that this is of, and the other foure are somewhat lesse: and I send them all painted vnto your lordship with the voyage. And the parchment wherein the picture is, was found here with other parchments. The people of this towne seeme vnto me of a reasonable stature, and wittie, yet they seeme not to bee such as they should bee, of that judgement and wit to builde these houses in such sort as they are.

For the most part they goe all naked, except their priuie partes which are couered; and they haue painted mantles like those which I send vnto your lordship. They haue no cotton wooll growing, because the countrey is colde, yet they weare mantels thereof as your honour may see by the shewe thereof: and true it is that there was found in their houses certaine yarne made of cotton wooll. They weare their haire on their heads like those of Mexico, and they are well nurtured and condicioned: And they haue Turqueses I thinke good quantitie, which with the rest of the goods which they had, except their corne, they had conueyed away before I came thither: for I found no women there, nor no youth vnder flfteene yeeres olde, nor no olde folkes aboue sixtie, sauing two or three olde folkes, who stayed behinde to gouerne all the rest of the youth and men of warre. There were found in a certaine paper two poynts of Emralds, and certaine small stones broken which are in colour somewhat like Granates very bad, and other stones of Christall, which I gaue one of my seruaunts to lay vp to send them to your lordship, and hee hath lost them as hee telleth me. We found heere Guinie cockes, but fewe. The Indians tell mee in all these seuen cities, that they eate them not, but that they keepe them onely for their feathers. I beleeue them not, for they are excellent good, and greater then those of Mexico. The season which is in this countrey, and the temperature of the ayre is like that of Mexico: for sometime it is hotte, and sometime it raineth: but hitherto I neuer sawe it raine, but once there fell a little showre with winde, as they are woont to fall in Spaine.

The snow and cold are woont to be great, for so say the inhabitants of the Countrey: and it is very likely so to bee, both in respect to the maner of the Countrey, and by the fashion of their houses, and their furres and other things which this people haue to defend them from colde. There is no kind of fruit nor trees of fruite. The Countrey is all plaine, and is on no side mountainous: albeit there are some hillie and bad passages. There are small store of Foules: the cause whereof is the colde, and because the mountaines are not neere. Here is no great store of wood, because they haue wood for their fuell sufficient foure leagues off from a wood of small Cedars. There is most excellent grasse within a quarter of a league hence, for our horses as well to feede them in pasture, as to mowe and make hay, whereof wee stoode in great neede, because our horses came hither so weake and feeble. The victuals which the people of this countrey haue, is Maiz, whereof they haue great store, and also small white Pease: and Venison, which by all likelyhood they feede vpon, (though they say no) for wee found many skinnes of Deere, of Hares, and Conies. They eate the best cakes that euer I sawe, and euery body generally eateth of them. They haue the finest order and way to grinde that wee euer sawe in any place. And one Indian woman of this countrey will grinde as much as foure women of Mexico. They haue most excellent salte in kernell, which they fetch from a certaine lake a dayes iourney from hence....

The kingdome of Totonteac so much extolled by the Father prouinciall, which sayde that there were such wonderfull things there, and such great matters, and that they made cloth there, the Indians say is an hotte lake, about which are fiue or sixe houses; and that there were certaine other, but that they are ruinated by warre. The kingdome of Marata is not to be found, neither haue the Indians any knowledge thereof. The kingdome of Acus is one onely small citie, where they gather cotton which is called Acucu. This is a town whereinto the kingdom of Acus is conuerted. Beyond this towne they say there are other small townes which are neere to a riuer which I haue seene and haue had report of by the relation of the Indians. I would to God I had better newes to write vnto your lordship: neuerthelesse, I must say the trueth: And as I wrote to your lordship from Culiacan, I am nowe to aduertise your honour as wel of the good as of the bad. Yet this I would haue you bee assured, that if all the riches and the treasures of the world were heere, I could haue done no more in the seruice of his Maiestie and of your lordshippe, than I haue done in comming hither whither you haue sent mee, my selfe and my companions carrying our victuals vpon our shoulders and vpon our horses three hundred leagues; and many dayes going on foote trauailing ouer hilles and rough mountaines, with other troubles which I cease to mention, neither purpose I to depart vnto the death, if it please his Maiestie and your lordship that it shall be so.

Three dayes after this citie was taken, certaine Indians of these people came to offer mee peace, and brought mee certaine Turqueses, and badde mantles, and I receiued them in his Maiesties name with all the good speaches that I could deuise, certifying them of the purpose of my comming into this countrey, which is in the name of his Maiestie, and by the commaundement of your Lordship, that they and all the rest of the people of this prouince should become Christians, and should knowe the true God for their Lorde, and receiue his Maiestie for their King and earthly Soueraigne: And herewithall they returned to their houses, and suddenly the next day they set in order all their goods and substance, their women and children, and fled to the hilles, leauing their townes as it were abandoned, wherein remained very fewe of them. When I sawe this within eight or tennes dayes after being recouered of my woundes, I went to the citie, which I sayde to bee greater then this where I am, and found there some fewe of them, to whom I sayde that they should not be afrayd, and that they should call their gouernour vnto mee: Howbeit forasmuch as I can learne or gather, none of them hath any gouernour: for I sawe not there any chiefe house, whereby any preeminence of one ouer another might bee gathered.

I would haue sent your lordshippe with this dispatch many musters of things which are in this countrey: but the way is so long and rough, that it is hard for me to doe so; neuerthelesse I send you twelue small mantles, such as the people of the countrey are woont to weare, and a certaine garment also, which seemeth vnto me to bee well made: I kept the same, because it seemed to mee to bee excellent well wrought, because I beleeue that no man euer sawe any needle worke in these Indies, except it were since the Spaniards inhabited the same. I send your Lordshippe also two clothes painted with the beasts of this countrey, although as I haue sayde, the picture bee very rudely done, because the painter spent but one day in drawing of the same. I haue seene other pictures on the walles of the houses of this citie with farre better proportion, and better made.

I send your honour one Oxe-hide, certaine Turqueses, and two earerings of the same, and fifteene combes of the Indians, and certain tablets set with these Turqueses, and two small baskets made of wicker, whereof the Indians haue great store. I send your lordship also two rolles which the women in these parts are woont to weare on their heads when they fetch water from their welles, as wee vse to doe in Spaine. And one of these Indian women with one of these rolles on her head, will carie a pitcher of water without touching the same with her hand vp a lather. I send you also a muster of the weapons wherewith these people are woont to fight, a buckler, a mace, a bowe, and certaine arrowes, among which are two with points of bones, the like whereof, as these conquerours say, haue neuer beene seene.

THE DISCOVERY OF THE MISSISSIPPI BY DE SOTO (1541)

PARKMAN'S ACCOUNT [1]

Hernando de Soto was the companion of Pizarro in the conquest of Peru. He had come to America a needy adventurer, with no other fortune than his sword and target. But his exploits had given him fame and fortune, and he appeared at court with the retinue of a nobleman. Still, his active energies could not endure repose, and his avarice and ambition goaded him to fresh enterprises. He asked and obtained permission to conquer Florida. While this design was in agitation, Cabeça de Vaca, one of those who had survived the expedition of Narvaez, appeared in Spain, and for purposes of his own, spread abroad the mischievous falsehood that Florida was the richest country yet discovered. De Soto's plans were embraced with enthusiasm. Nobles and gentlemen contended for the privilege of joining his standard; and, setting sail with an ample armament, he landed at the Bay of Espiritu Santo, now Tampa Bay, in Florida, with six hundred and twenty chosen men, a band as gallant and well appointed, as eager in purpose and audacious in hope, as ever trod the shores of the New World. The clangor of trumpets, the neighing of horses, the fluttering of pennons, the glittering of helmet and lance, startled the ancient forest with unwonted greeting. Amid this pomp of chivalry, religion was not forgotten. The sacred vessels and vestments with bread and wine for the Eucharist were carefully provided; and De Soto himself declared that the enterprise was undertaken for God alone, and seemed to be the object of His especial care. These devout marauders could not neglect the spiritual welfare of the Indians whom they had come to plunder; and besides fetters to bind, and bloodhounds to hunt them, they brought priests and monks for the saving of their souls.

The adventurers begun their march. Their story has been often told. For month after month and year after year, the procession of priests and cavaliers, crossbowmen, arquebusiers, and Indian captives laden with the baggage, still wandered on through wild and boundless wastes, lured hither and thither by the ignis-fatuus of their hopes. They traversed great portions of Georgia, Alabama, and Mississippi, everywhere inflicting and enduring misery, but never approaching their fantom El Dorado. At length, in the third year of their journeying, they reached the banks of the Mississippi, a hundred and thirty-two years before its second discovery by Marquette. One of their number describes the great river as almost half a league wide, deep, rapid, and constantly rolling down trees and drift-wood on its turbid current.

The Spaniards crossed over at a point above the mouth of the Arkansas. They advanced westward, but found no treasures—nothing, indeed, but hardships, and an Indian enemy, furious, writes one of their officers, "as mad dogs." They heard of a country toward the north where maize could not be cultivated because the vast herds of wild cattle devoured it. [2] They penetrated so far that they entered the range of the roving prairie tribes; for, one day, as they pushed their way with difficulty across great plains covered with tall, rank grass, they met a band of savages who dwelt in lodges of skins sewed together, subsisting on game alone, and wandering perpetually from place to place. Finding neither gold nor the South Sea, for both of which they had hoped, they returned to the banks of the Mississippi.

De Soto, says one of those who accompanied him, was a "stern man, and of few words." Even in the midst of reverses, his will had been law to his followers, and he had sustained himself through the depths of disappointment with the energy of a stubborn pride. But his hour was come. He fell into deep dejection, followed by an attack of fever, and soon after died miserably. To preserve his body from the Indians, his followers sank it at midnight in the river, and the sullen waters of the Mississippi buried his ambition and his hopes.

The adventurers were now, with few exceptions, disgusted with the enterprise, and longed only to escape from the scene of their miseries. After a vain attempt to reach Mexico by Land, they again turned back to the Mississippi, and labored, with all the resources which their desperate necessity could suggest, to construct vessels in which they might make their way to some Christian settlement. Their condition was most forlorn. Few of their horses remained alive; their baggage had been destroyed at the burning of the Indian town of Mavila, and many of the soldiers were without armor and without weapons. In place of the gallant array which, more than three years before, had left the harbor of Espiritu Santo, a company of sickly and starving men were laboring among the swampy forests of the Mississippi, some clad in skins, and some in mats woven from a kind of wild vine.

Seven brigantines were finished and launched; and, trusting their lives on board these frail vessels, they descended the Mississippi, running the gantlet between hostile tribes, who fiercely attacked them. Reaching the Gulf, tho not without the loss of eleven of their number, they made sail for the Spanish settlement on the River Panuco, where they arrived safely, and where the inhabitants met them with a cordial welcome. Three hundred and eleven men thus escaped with life, leaving behind them the bones of their comrades strewn broadcast through the wilderness.

THE DEATH OF DE SOTO (1542)

BY ONE OF DE SOTO'S COMPANIONS [1]

The Governor fell into great dumps to see how hard it was to get to the sea; and worse, because his men and horses every day diminished, being without succor to sustain themselves in the country: and with that thought he fell sick. But before he took his bed he sent an Indian to the Cacique of Quigalta to tell him that he was the child of the sun, and that all the way that he came all men obeyed and served him, that he requested him to accept of his friendship and come unto him, for he would be very glad to see him; and in sign of love and obedience to bring something with him of that which in his country was most esteemed....

By the time the Indian returned with his answer, the Governor had betaken himself to bed, being evil handled with fevers, and was much aggrieved that he was in case to pass presently the river and to seek him, to see if he could abate that pride of his, considering the river went now very strongly in those parts; for it was near half a league broad, and sixteen fathoms deep, and very furious, and ran with a great current; and on both sides there were many Indians, and his power was not now so great, but that he had need to help himself rather by slights than by force. The Indians of Guachoya came every day with fish in such numbers, that the town was full of them....

The Governor felt in himself that the hour approached wherein he was to leave this present life, and called for the king's officers, captains, and principal persons, to whom he made a speech. Baltasar de Gallegos answered in the name of all the rest. And first of all comforting him, he set before his eyes how short the life of this world was, and with how many troubles and miseries it is accompanied, and how God showed him a singular favor which soonest left it: telling him many other things fit for such a time. And touching the Governor which he commanded they should elect, he besought him, that it would please his lordship to name him which he thought fit, and him they would obey. And presently he named Luys de Moscoso de Alvarado, his captain-general. And presently he was sworn by all that were present, and elected for governor. The next day being the 21st of May, 1542, departed out of this life the valorous, virtuous, and valiant captain, Don Fernando de Soto, Governor of Cuba, and Adelantado of Florida: whom fortune advanced, as it useth to do others, that he might have the higher fall. He departed in such a place, and at such a time, as in his sickness he had but little comfort: and the danger wherein all his people were of perishing in that country, which appeared before their eyes, was cause sufficient why every one of them had need of comfort, and why they did not visit nor accompany him as they ought to have done. Luys de Moscoso determined to conceal his death from the Indians, because Fernando de Soto had made them believe that the Christians were immortal; and also because they took him to be hardy, wise, and valiant; and if they should know that he was dead, they would be bold to set upon the Christians, tho they lived peaceably by them.

As soon as he was dead, Luys de Moscoso commanded to put him secretly in the house, where he remained three days; and moving him from thence, commanded him to be buried in the night at one of the gates of the town within the wall. And as the Indians had seen him sick, and missed him, so did they suspect what might be. And passing by the place where he was buried, seeing the earth moved, they looked and spake one to another. Luys de Moscoso, understanding of it, commanded him to be taken up by night, and to cast a great deal of sand into the mantles, wherein he was wound up, wherein he was carried in a canoe, and thrown into the midst of the river.

The Cacique of Guachoya inquired for him, demanding what was become of his brother and lord, the Governor. Luys de Moscoso told him that he was gone to heaven, as many other times he did: and because he was to stay there certain days he had left him in his place. The cacique thought with himself that he was dead; and commanded two young and well-proportioned Indians to be brought thither; and said, that the use of that country was, when any lord died, to kill Indians to wait upon him, and serve him by the way, and for that purpose by his commandment were those come thither: and prayed Luys de Moscoso to command them to be beheaded, that they might attend and serve his lord and brother. Luys de Moscoso told him that the Governor was not dead, but gone to heaven, and that of his own Christian soldiers he had taken such as he needed to serve him, and prayed him to command those Indians to be loosed, and not to use any such bad custom from thenceforth: straightway he commanded them to be loosed, and to get them home to their houses.

DRAKE'S VISIT TO CALIFORNIA (1579)

BY ONE OF DRAKE'S COMPANIONS [1]

From Guatulco we departed the day following, viz, Aprill 16, [1579] setting our course directly into the sea, whereon we sayled 500 leagues in longitude, to get a winde: and between that and June 3, 1400 leagues in all, till we came into 42 deg. of North latitude, where in the night following we found such alteration of heate, into extreame and nipping cold, that our men in generall did grieuously complaine thereof, some of them feeling their healths much impaired thereby; neither was it that this chanced in the night alone, but the day following carried with it not onely the markes, but the stings and force of the night going before, to the great admiration of vs all; for besides that the pinching and biting aire was nothing altered, the very roapes of our ship were stiffe, and the raine which fell was an unnatural congealed and frozen substance, so that we seemed rather to be in the frozen Zone then any way so neere vnto the sun, or these hotter climates....

The 3 day following, uiz., the 21, our ship hauing receiued a leake at sea, was brought to anchor neerer the shoare, that, her goods being landed, she might be repaired; but for that we were to preuent any danger that might chance against our safety, our Generall first of all landed his men, with all necessary prouision, to build tents and make a fort for the defence of our selues and goods: and that wee might vnder the shelter of it with more safety (what euer should befall) end our businesse; which when the people of the countrey perceiued vs doing, as men set on fire to war in defence of their countrie, in great hast and companies, with such weapons as they had, they came downe vnto vs, and yet with no hostile meaning or intent to hurt vs: standing, when they drew neere, as men rauished in their mindes, with the sight of such things as they neuer had seene or heard of before that time: their errand being rather with submission and feare to worship vs as Gods, then to haue any warre with vs as with mortall men, which thing, as it did partly shew itself at that instant, so did it more and more manifest itself afterwards, during the whole time of our abode amongst them. At this time, being willed by signes to lay from them their bowes and arrowes, they did as they were directed, and so did all the rest, as they came more and more by companies vnto them, growing in a little while to a great number, both of men and women.

To the intent, therefore, that this peace which they themselues so willingly sought might, without any cause of the breach thereof on our part given, be continued, and that wee might with more safety and expedition end our businesses in quiet, our Generall, with all his company, vsed all meanes possible gently to intreate them, bestowing vpon each of them liberally good and necessary things to couer their nakednesse; withall signifying vnto them we were no Gods, but men, and had neede of such things to couer our owns shame; teaching them to vse them to the same ends, for which cause also wee did eate and drinke in their presence, giuing them to vnderstand that without that wee could not liue, and therefore were but men as well as they.

Notwithstanding nothing could perswade them, nor remoue that opinion which they had conceiued of vs, that wee should be Gods.

In recompence of those things which they had receiued of vs, as shirts, linnen cloth, etc., they bestowed vpon our Generall, and diuerse of our company, diuerse things, as feathers, cawles of networke, the quiuers of their arrowes, made of fawne skins, and the very skins of beasts that their women wore vpon their bodies. Hauing thus had their fill of this times visiting and beholding of vs, they departed with ioy to their houses, which houses are digged round within the earth, and haue from the vppermost brimmes of the circle clefts of wood set vp, and ioyned close together at the top, like our spires on the steeple of a Church; which being couered with earth, suffer no water to enter, and are very warme; the doore in the most part of them performes the office also of a chimney to let out the smoake: its made in bignesse and fashion like to an ordinary scuttle in a ship, and standing slopewise: their beds are the hard ground, onely with rushes strewed vpon it, and lying round about the house, haue their fire in the middest, which by reason that the house is but low vaulted, round, and close, giueth a maruelous reflexion to their bodies to heate the same.

Their men for the most part goe naked; the women take a kinde of bulrushes, and kembing it after the manner of hemp, make themselues thereof a loose garment, which being knitte about their middles, hanges downe about their hippes, and so affordes to them a couering of that which nature teaches should be hidden; about their shoulders they weare also the skin of a deere, with the haire vpon it. They are very obedient to their husbands, and exceeding ready in all seruices; yet of themselues offring to do nothing, without the consents or being called of the men....

Against the end of three daies more (the newes hauing the while spread itselfe farther, and as it seemed a great way vp into the countrie), were assembled the greatest number of people which wee could reasonably imagine to dwell within any conuenient distance round about. Amongst the rest the king himselfe, a man of a goodly stature and comely personage, attended with his guard of about 100 tall and warlike men, this day, viz., June 26, came downe to see vs.

Before his comming, were sent two embassadors or messengers to our Generall, to signifie that their Hioh, that is, their king, was comming and at hand. They in the deliuery of their message, the one spake with a soft and low voice, prompting his fellow; the other pronounced the same, word by word, after him with a voice more audible, continuing their proclamation (for such it was) about halfe an houre. Which being ended, they by signes made request to our Generall, to send something by their hands to their Hioh or king, as a token that his comming might be in peace. Our Generall willingly satisfied their desire; and they, glad men, made speedy returne to their Hioh. Neither was it long before their king (making as princely a shew as possibly he could) with all his traine came forward.

In their comining forwards they cryed continually after a singing manner, with a lustie courage. And as they drew neerer and neerer towards vs, so did they more and more striue to behaue themselues with a certaine comelinesse and grauity in all their actions.

In the forefront came a man of a large body and goodly aspect, bearing the Scepter or royall mace, made of a certaine kind of blacke wood, and in length about a yard and a halfe, before the king. Whereupon hanged two crownes, a bigger and a lesser, with three chaines of a maruellous length, and often doubled, besides a bagge of the herbe Tabáh. The crownes were made of knitworke, wrought vpon most curiously with feathers of diners colours, very artificially placed, and of a formall fashion. The chaines seemed of a bony substance, euery linke or part thereof being very little, thinne, most finely burnished, with a hole pierced through the middest. The number of linkes going to make one chaine is in a manner infinite; but of such estimation it is amongst them, that few be the persons that are admitted to weare the same; and euen they to whom its lawfull to use them, yet are stinted what number they shall vse, as some ten, some twelue, some twentie, and as they exceed in number of chaines, so thereby are they knowne to be the more honorable personages.

Next vnto him that bare this Scepter was the king himselfe with his guard about him; his attire vpon his head was a cawle of knitworke, wrought vpon somewhat like the crownes, but differing much both in fashion and perfectnesse of worke; vpon his shoulders he had on a coate of the skins of conies, reaching to his wast; his guard also had each coats of the same shape, but of other skins; some hauing cawles likewise stucke with feathers, or couered ouer with a certaine downe, which groweth vp in the countrey vpon an herbe much like our lectuce, which exceeds any other downe in the world for finenesse, and being layed vpon their cawles, by no winds can be remoued....

In the meane time, our Generall hauing assembled his men together (as forecasting the danger and worst that might fall out) prepared himselfe to stand vpon sure ground, that wee might at all times be ready in our owne defence, if any thing should chance otherwise than was looked for or expected.

Wherefore euery man being in a warlike readinesse, he marched within his fenced place, making against their approach a most warlike shew (as he did also at all other times of their resort), whereby if they had beene desperate enemies, they could not haue chosen but haue conceiued terrour and fear, with discouragement to attempt anything against vs, in beholding of the same.

When they were come somewhat neere vnto vs, trooping together, they gaue vs a common or generall salutation, observing in the meane time a generall silence. Whereupon, he who bare the Scepter before the king, being prompted by another whom the king assigned to that office, pronounced with an audible and manly voice what the other spake to him in secret, continuing, whether it were his oration or proclamation, at the least halfe an houre. At the close whereof there was a common Amen, in signe of approbation, giuen by euery person: and the king himselfe, with the whole number of men and women (the little children onely remaining behind) came further downe the hill, and as they came set themselues againe in their former order.

And beeing now come to the foot of the hill and neere our fort, the Scepter bearer, with a composed countenance and stately carriage began a song, and answerable thereunto obserued a kind of measures in a dance: whom the king with his guard and euery other sort of person following, did in like manner sing and daunce, sauing onely the women, who danced but kept silence. As they danced they still came on: and our Generall perceiuing their plaine and simple meaning, gaue order that they might freely enter without interruption within our bulwarke. Where, after they had entred, they yet continued their song and dance a reasonable time, their women also following them with their wassaile boales in their hands, their bodies bruised, their faces tome, their dugges, breasts, and other parts bespotted with bloud, trickling downe from the wounds, which with their nailes they had made before their comming.

After that they had satisfied, or rather tired themselues in this manner, they made signes to our Generall to haue him sit down; unto whom both the king and diuers others made seuerall orations, or rather, indeed, if wee had vnderstood them, supplications, that hee would take the Prouince and kingdome into his hand, and become their king and patron: making signes that they would resigne vnto him their right and title in the whole land, and become his vassals in themselues and their posterities: which that they might make vs indeed beleeue that it was their true meaning and intent, the king himselfe, with all the rest, with one consent and with great reuerence, ioyfully singing a song, set the crowne vpon his head, inriched his necke with all their chaines, and offering vnto him many other things, honoured him by the name of Hyoh. Adding thereunto (as it might seeme) a song and dance of triumph; because they were not onely visited of the gods (for so they still iudged vs to be), but the great and chiefe God was now become their God, their king and patron, and themselues were become the onely happie and blessed people in the world.

These things being so freely offered, our Generall thought not meet to reject or refuse the same, both for that he would not giue them any cause of mistrust or disliking of him (that being the onely place, wherein at this present, we were of necessitie inforced to seeke reliefe of many things), and chiefely for that he knew not to what good end God had brought this to passe, or what honour and profit it might bring to our countrie in time to come.

Wherefore, in the name and to the vse of her most excellent majesty, he tooke the scepter, crowue, and dignity of the sayd countrie into his hand; wishing nothing more than that it had layen so fitly for her maiesty to enioy, as it was now her proper owne, and that the riches and treasures thereof (wherewith in the vpland countries it abounds) might with as great conueniency be transported, to the enriching of her kingdome here at home, as it is in plenty to be attained there; and especially that so tractable and louing a people as they shewed themselues to be, might haue meanes to haue manifested their most willing obedience the more vnto her, and by her meanes, as a mother and nurse of the Church of Christ, might by the preaching of the Gospell, be brought to the right knowledge and obedience of the true and euerliuing God.

The ceremonies of this resigning and receiving of the kingdome being thus performed, the common sort, both of men and women, leauing the king and his guard about him, with out Generall, dispersed themselues among our people, taking a diligent view or suruey of euery man; and finding such as pleased their fancies (which commonly were the youngest of vs), they presently enclosing them about offred their sacrifices vnto them, crying out with lamentable shreekes and moanes, weeping and scratching and tearing their very flesh off their faces with their nailes; neither were it the women alone which did this, but euen old men, roaring and crying out, were as violent as the women were.

Few were the dayes, wherein they were absent from vs, during the whole time of our abode in that place; and ordinarily euery third day they brought their sacrifices, till such time as they certainely vnderstood our meaning, that we tooke no pleasure, but were displeased with them; whereupon their zeale abated, and their sacrificing, for a season, to our good liking ceased; notwithstanding they continued still to make their resort vnto vs in great abundance, and in such sort, that they oft-time forgate to prouide meate for their owne sustenance....

This country our Generall named Albion, and that for two causes; the one in respect of the white bancks and cliffes, which lie toward the sea; the other, that it might haue some affinity, euen in name also, with our own country which was sometime so called.

Before we went from thence, our Generall caused to be set vp a monument of our being there, as also of her maiesties and successors right and title to that kingdome; namely, a plate of brasse, fast nailed to a great and firme poste; whereon is engrauen her graces name, and the day and yeare of our arriuall there, and of the free guing vp of the prouince and kingdome, both by the king and people, into her majesties hands: together with her highnesse picture and armes, in a piece of sixpence currant English monie, shewing itselfe by a hole made of purpose through the plate; vnderneath was likewise engrauen the name of our Generall, etc.

The Spaniards neuer had any dealing, or so much as set a foote in this country, the vtmost of their discoueries reaching onely to many degrees Southward of this place.

And now, as the time of our departure was perceiued by them to draw nigh, so did the sorrowes and miseries of this people seeme to themselues to increase vpon them, and the more certaine they were of our going away, the more doubtfull they shewed themselues what they might doe; so that we might easily iudge that that ioy (being exceeding great) wherewith they receiued vs at our first arriuall, was cleane drowned in their excessiue sorrow for our departing. For they did not only loose on a sudden all mirth, ioy, glad countenance, pleasant speeches, agility of body, familiar rejoycing one with another, and all pleasure what euer flesh and blood might bee delighted in, but with sighes and sorrowings, with heauy hearts and grieued minds, they powred out wofull complaints and moanes, with bitter teares and wringing of their hands, tormenting themselues. And as men refusing all comfort, they onely accounted themselues as cast-awayes, and those whom the gods were about to forsake: so that nothing we could say or do, was able to ease them of their so heauy a hurthen, or to deliuer them from so desperate a straite, as our leauing of them did seeme to them that it would cast them into....

The 23 of July they tooke a sorrowfull farewell of vs, but being loath to leaue vs, they presently ranne to the top of the hils to keepe vs in their sight as long as they could, making fires before and behind, and on each side of them, burning therein (as is to be supposed) sacrifices at our departure.

HUDSON'S DISCOVERY OF THE HUDSON RIVER (1609)

BY ROBERT JUET, HUDSON'S SECRETARY [1]

The first of September [1609], faire weather, the wind variable betweene east and south; we steered away north northwest. At noone we found our height to bee 39 degrees, 3 minutes. The second, in the morning, close weather, the winde at south in the morning; from twelve untill two of the clocke we steered north northwest, and had sounding one and twentie fathoms: and in running one glasse we had but sixteene fathoms, then seventeene, and so shoalder and shoalder untill it came to twelve fathoms. We saw a great fire, but could not see the land; then we came to ten fathoms, whereupon we brought our tackes aboord, and stood to the eastward east south-east, foure glasses. Then the sunne arose, and wee steered away north againe, and saw the land from the west by north to the northwest by north, all like broken islands, [2] and our soundings were eleven and ten fathoms. Then wee looft in for the shoare, and faire by the shoare we had seven fathoms. The course along the land we found to be northeast by north. From the land which we had first sight of, untill we came to a great lake of water, as wee could judge it to bee, being drowned land, which made it to rise like islands, which was in length ten leagues. The mouth of that land hath many shoalds, and the sea breaketh on them as it is cast out of the mouth of it. And from that lake or bay the land lyeth north by east, and wee had a great streame out of the bay; and from thence our sounding was ten fathoms two leagues from the land. At five of the clocke we anchored, being little winde, and rode in eight fathoms water; the night was faire. This night I found the land to hail the compasse 8 degrees. For to the northward off us we saw high hils. For the day before we found not above 2 degrees of variation. This is a very good land to fall with, and a pleasant land to see.

The third, the morning mystie, untill ten of the clocke; then it cleered, and the wind came to the south south-east, so wee weighed and stood to the northward. The land [3] is very pleasant and high, and bold to fall withall. At three of the clock in the after-noone, wee came to three great rivers. So we stood along to the northermost, thinking to have gone into it, but we found it to have a very shoald barre before it, for we had but ten foot water. Then we cast about to the southward, and found two fathoms, three fathoms, and three and a quarter, till we came to the souther side of them; then we had five and six fathoms, and anchored.

The fourth, in the morning, as soone as the day was light, wee saw that it was good riding farther up. So we sent out boate to sound, and found that it was a very good harbour, and foure and five fathomes, two cables length from the shoare. Then we weighed and went in with our ship. Then our boate went on land [4] with our net to fish, and caught ten great mullets, of a foote and a halfe long a peese, and a ray as great as foure men could hale into the ship. So wee trimmed our boate and rode still all day. At night the wind blew hard at the north-west, and our anchor came home, and we drove on shoare, but took no hurt, thanked bee God, for the ground is soft sand and oze. This day the people of the countrey came aboord of us, seeming very glad of our comming, and brought greene tobacco, and gave us of it for knives and beads. They goe in deere skins loose, well dressed. They have yellow copper. They desire cloathes, and are very civill. They have great store of maize, or Indian wheate, whereof they make good bread. The countrey is full of great and tall oake.

The fifth, in the morning, as soone as the day was light, the wind ceased and the flood came. So we heaved off our ship againe into five fathoms water, and sent our boate to sound the bay, and we found that there was three fathoms hard by the souther shoare. Our men went on land there, and saw great store of men, women, and children, who gave them tabacco at their comming on land. So they went up into the woods, and saw great store of very goodly oakes and some currants. For one of them came aboord and brought some dryed, and gave me some, which were sweet and good. This day many of the people came aboard, some in mantles of feathers, and some in skinnes of divers sorts of good furres. Some women also came to us with hempe. They had red copper tabacco pipes, and other things of copper they did weare about their neckes. At night they went on land againe, so wee rode very quiet, but durst not trust them.

The sixth, in the morning, was faire weather, and our master sent John Colman, with foure other men in our boate, over to the north-side to sound the other river [5] , being foure leagues from us. They found by the day shoald water, two fathoms; but at the north of the river eighteen, and twentie fathoms, and very good riding for ships; and a narrow river to the westward, between two ilands. The lands, they told us, were as pleasant with grasse and flowers and goodly trees as ever they had seene, and very sweet smells came from them....

The tenth, faire weather, we rode still till twelve of the clocke. Then we weighed and went over, and found it shoald all the middle of the river, for wee could finde but two fathoms and a halfe and three fathomes for the space of a league; then wee came to three fathomes and foure fathomes, and so to seven fathomes, and anchored, and rode all night in soft ozie ground. The banke is sand.

The eleventh was faire and very hot weather. At one of the clocke in the after-noone wee weighed and went into the river, the wind at south south-west, little winde. Our soundings were seven, sixe, five, sixe, seven, eight, nine, ten, twelve, thirteene, and fourteene fathomes. Then it shoalded againe, and came to five fathomes. Then wee anchored, and saw that it was a very good harbour for all windes, and rode all night. The people of the country came aboord of us, making shew of love, and gave us tabacco and Indian wheat, and departed for that night, but we durst not trust them.

The twelfth, very faire and hot. In the afternoone, at two of the clocke, wee weighed, the winde being variable betweene the north and the north-west. So we turned into the river two leagues and anchored. This morning, at our first rode in the river, there came eight and twentie canoes full of men, women and children to betray us: but we saw their intent, and suffered none of them to come aboord of us. At twelve of the clocke they departed. They brought with them oysters and beanes, whereof wee bought some. They have great tabacco pipes of yellow copper, and pots of earth to dresse their meate in. It floweth south-east by south within.

The thirteenth, faire weather, the wind northerly. At seven of the clocke in the morning, as the floud came we weighed, and turned foure miles into the river. The tide being done wee anchored. Then there came foure canoes aboord: but we suffered none of them to come into our ship. They brought great store of very good oysters aboord, which we bought for trifles. [6] In the night I set the variation of the compasse, and found it to be 13 degrees. In the after-noone we weighed, and turned in with the floud, two leagues and a halfe further, and anchored all night; and had five fathoms soft ozie ground; and had an high point of land, which shewed out to us, bearing north by east five leagues off us.

The fourteenth, in the morning, being very faire weather, the wind south-east, we sayled up the river twelve leagues, and had five fathoms, and five fathoms and a quarter lesse; and came to a streight betweene two points, [7] and had eight, nine, and ten fathoms; and it attended north-east by north, one league: and wee had twelve, thirteene, and fourteene fathomes. The river is a mile broad: there is very high land on both sides. Then we went up north-west, a league and an halfe deepe water. Then north-east by north, five miles; then north-west by north, two leagues, and anchored. The land grew very high and mountainous. The river is full of fish.

The fifteenth, in the morning, was misty, untill the sunne arose: then it cleered. So wee weighed with the wind at south, and ran up into the river twentie leagues, passing by high mountaines. [8] Wee had a very good depth, as sixe, seven, eight, nine, ten, twelve, and thirteene fathomes, and great store of salmons in the river. This morning our two savages got out of a port and swam away. I After wee were under sayle, they called to us in scorne. At night we came to other mountaines, which lie from the rivers side. There wee found very loving people, and very old men: where wee were well used. Our boat went to fish, and caught great store of very good fish....

The seventeenth, faire sun-shining weather, and very hot. In the morning, as soone as the sun was up, we set sayle, and ran up six leagues higher, and found shoalds in the middle of the channell, and small ilands, but seven fathoms water on both sides. Toward night we borrowed so neere the shoare, that we grounded: so layed out our small anchor, and heaved off againe. Then we borrowed on the banke in the channell, and came aground againe; while the floud ran we heaved off againe, and anchored all night. [9]

The eighteenth, in the morning, was faire weather, and we rode still. In the after-noone our masters mate went on land with an old savage, a governor of the countrey; who carried him to his house, and made him good cheere. The nineteenth, was faire and hot weather: at the floud, being neere eleven of the clocke, wee weighed, and ran higher up two leagues above the shoalds, and had no lesse water then five fathoms; we anchored, and rode in eight fathomes. The people of the countrie came flocking aboord, and brought us grapes and pompions, which wee bought for trifles. And many brought us bevers skinnes and otters skinnes, which wee bought for beades, knives, and hatchets. So we rode there all night.

The twentieth, in the morning, was faire weather. Our masters mate with foure men more went up with our boat to sound the river, and found two leagues above us but two fathomes water, and the channell very narrow; and above that place, seven or eight fathomes. Toward night they returned: and we rode still all night. The one and twentieth was faire weather, and the wind all southerly: we determined yet once more to go farther up into the river, to trie what depth and breadth it did beare; but much people resorted aboord, so wee went not this day. Our carpenter went on land, and made a fore-yard. And our master and his mate determined to trie some of the chiefe men of the countrey, whether they had any treaeherie in them. So they tooke them downe into the cabin, and gave them so much wine and aqua vita, that they were all merrie: and one of them had his wife with them, which sate so modestly, as any of our countrey women would doe in a strange place. In the ende one of them was drunke, which had beene aboord of our ship all the time that we had beene there: and that was strange to them; for they could not tell how to take it. The canoes and folke went all on shoare: but some of them came againe, and brought stropes of beades: some had sixe, seven, eight, nine, ten; and gave him. So he slept all night quietly.

The two and twentieth was faire weather: in the morning our masters mate and foure more of the companie went up with our boat to sound the river higher up. The people of the countrey came not aboord till noone: but when they came, and saw the savages well, they were glad. So at three of the clocke in the afternoone they came aboord, and brought tabacco, and more beades, and gave them to our master, and made an oration, and shewed him all the countrey round about. Then they sent one of their companie on land, who presently returned, and brought a great platter full of venison dressed by themselves; and they caused him to eate with them: then they made him reverence and departed, all save the old man that lay aboord. This night, at ten of the clocke our boat returned in a showre of raine from sounding of the river; and found it to bee at an end for shipping to goe in. For they had beene up eight or nine leagues, and found but seven foot water, and unconstant soundings.

The three and twentieth, faire weather. At twelve of the clocke wee weighed, and went downe two leagues to a shoald that had two channels, one on the one side, and another on the other, and had little wind, whereby the tyde layed us upon it. So there wee sate on ground the space of an houre till the floud came. Then we had a little gale of wind at the west. So wee got our ship into deepe water, and rode all night very well.

The foure and twentieth was faire weather: the winde at the north-west, wee weighed, and went downe the river seven or eight leagues; and at halfe ebbe wee came on ground on a banke of oze in the middle of the river, and sate there till the floud. Then wee went on land, and gathered, good store of chest-nuts. At ten of the clocke wee came off into deepe water, and anchored....

The second, faire weather. At break of day wee weighed, the winde being at north-west, and got downe seven leagues; then the floud was come strong, so we anchored. Then came one of the savages that swamme away from us at our going up the river with many other, thinking to betray us. But we perceived their intent, and suffered none of them to enter our ship. Whereupon two canoes full of men, with their bowes and arrowes shot at us after our sterne: in recompence whereof we discharged sixe muskets, and killed two or three of them. Then above an hundred of them came to a point of land to shoot at us. There I shot a falcon at them, and killed two of them: whereupon the rest fled into the woods. Yet they manned off another canoe with nine or ten men, which came to meet us. So I shot at it also a falcon, and shot it through, and killed one of them. Then our men with their muskets killed three or foure more of them. [10] So they went their way; within a mile after wee got downe two leagues beyond that place, and anchored in a bay, cleere from all danger of them on the other side of the river, where we saw a very good piece of ground: and hard by it there was a cliffe, that looked of the colour of a white greene, as though it were either copper or silver myne: and I thinke it to be one of them, by the trees that grow upon it. For they be all burned, and the other places are greene as grasse; it is on that side of the river that is called Mannahata. There we saw no people to trouble us: and rode quietly all night; but had much wind and raine....

We continued our course toward England, without seeing any land by the way, all the rest of this moneth of October: and on the seventh day of November, stilo novo, being Saturday, by the grace of God we safely arrived in the range of Dartmouth, in Devonshire, in the yeere 1609.

CHAMPLAIN'S BATTLE WITH THE IROQUOIS ON LAKE CHAMPLAIN (1609)

BY CHAMPLAIN HIMSELF [1]

We continued our course to the entrance of Lake St. Peter, where the country is exceedingly pleasant and level, and crossed the lake, in two, three, and four fathoms of water, which is some eight leagues long and four wide. On the north side, we saw a very pleasant river, extending some twenty leagues into the interior, which I named St. Suzanne; on the south side, there are two, one called Rivière du Pont, the other Rivière de Gennes, which are very pretty, and in a fine and fertile country. The water is almost still in the lake, which is full of fish. On the north bank, there are seen some slight elevations at a distance of some twelve or fifteen leagues from the lake. After crossing the lake, we passed a large number of islands of various sizes, containing many nut trees and vines, and fine meadows, with quantities of game and wild animals, which go over from the main land to these islands. Fish are here more abundant than in any other part of the river that we have seen. From these islands, we went to the mouth of the River of the Iroquois, [2] where we stayed two days, refreshing ourselves with good venison, birds, and fish, which the savages gave us. Here there sprang up among them some difference of opinion on the subject of the war, so that a portion only determined to go with me, while the others returned to their country with their wives and the merchandise which they had obtained by barter.

I set out accordingly from the fall of the Iroquois River on the 2d of July. All the savages set to carrying their canoes, arms, and baggage overland, some half a league, in order to pass by the violence and strength of the fall, which was speedily accomplished....

We set out the next day, continuing our course in the river as far as the entrance of the lake. [3] There are many pretty islands here, low, and containing very fine woods and meadows, with abundance of fowl and such animals of the chase as stags, fallow-deer, fawns, roe-bucks, bears, and others, which go from the main land to these islands. We captured a large number of these animals. There are also many beavers, not only in this river, but also in numerous other little ones that flow into it. These regions, altho they are pleasant, are not inhabited by any savages, on account of their wars; but they withdraw as far as possible from the rivers into the interior, in order not to be suddenly surprised.

The next day we entered the lake, which is of great extent, say eighty or a hundred leagues long, where I saw four fine islands, ten, twelve, and fifteen leagues long, which were formerly inhabited by the savages, like the River of the Iroquois; but they have been abandoned since the wars of the savages with one another prevail. There are also many rivers falling into the lake, bordered by many fine trees of the same kinds as those we have in France, with many vines finer than any I have seen in any other place; also many chestnut-trees on the border of this lake, which I had not seen before....

Continuing our course over this lake on the western side, I noticed, while observing the country, some very high mountains on the eastern side, on the top of which there was snow. I made inquiry of the savages, whether these localities were inhabited, when they told me that the Iroquois dwelt there, and that there were beautiful valleys in these places, with plains productive in grain, such as I had eaten in this country, together with many kinds of fruit without limit. They said also that the lake extended near mountains, some twenty-five leagues distant from us, as I judge. I saw, on the south, other mountains no less high than the first, but without any snow. **[4]**

When it was evening, we embarked in our canoes to continue our course; and, as we advanced very quietly and without making any noise, we met on the 29th of the month the Iroquois, about ten o'clock at evening, at the extremity of a cape which extends into the lake on the western bank. They had come to fight. We both began to utter loud cries, all getting their arms in readiness. We withdrew out on the water, and the Iroquois went on shore, where they drew up all their canoes close to each other and began to fell trees with poor axes, which they acquire in war sometimes, using also others of stone. Thus they barricaded themselves very well.

Our forces also passed the entire night, their canoes being drawn up close to each other, and fastened to poles, so that they might not get separated, and that they might be all in readiness to fight, if occasion required.... After arming ourselves with light armor, we each took an arquebuse, and went on shore. I saw the enemy go out of their barricade, nearly two hundred in number, stout and rugged in appearance. They came at a slow pace toward us, with a dignity and assurance which greatly amused me, having three chiefs at their head. Our men also advanced in the same order, telling me that those who had three large plumes were the chiefs, and that they had only these three, and that they could be distinguished by these plumes, which were much larger than those of their companions, and that I should do what I could to kill them. I promised to do all in my power, and said that I was very sorry they could not understand me, so that I might give order and shape to their mode of attacking their enemies, and then we should, without doubt, defeat them all; but that this could not now be obviated, and that I should be very glad to show them my courage and good-will when we should engage in the fight.

As soon as we had landed, they began to run for some two hundred paces toward their enemies, who stood firmly, not having as yet noticed my companions, who went into the woods with some savages. Our men began to call me with loud cries; and in order to give me a passage-way, they opened in two parts, and put me at their head, where I marched some twenty paces in advance of the rest, until I was within about thirty paces of the enemy, who at once noticed me, and, halting, gazed at me, as I did also at them. When I saw them making a move to fire at us, I rested my musket against my cheek, and aimed directly at one of the three chiefs. With the same shot, two fell to the ground; and one of their men was so wounded that he died some time after. I had loaded my musket with four balls. When our side saw this shot so favorable for them, they began to raise such loud cries that one could not have heard it thunder. Meanwhile, the arrows flew on both sides. The Iroquois were greatly astonished that two men had been so quickly killed, altho they were equipped with armor woven from cotton thread, and with wood which was a proof against their arrows. This caused great alarm among them. As I was loading again, one of my companions fired a shot from the woods, which astonished them anew to such a degree that, seeing their chiefs dead, they lost courage, and took to flight, abandoning their camp and fort, and fleeing into the woods, whither I pursued them, killing still more of them. Our savages also killed several of them, and took ten or twelve prisoners. The remainder escaped with the wounded. Fifteen or sixteen were wounded on our side with arrow-shots; but they were soon healed.

After gaining the victory, our men amused themselves by taking a great quantity of Indian corn and some meal from their enemies, also their armor, which they had left behind that they might run better. After feasting sumptuously, dancing and singing, we returned three hours after, with the prisoners. The spot where this attack took place is in latitude 43 degrees and some minutes, and the lake was called Lake Champlain.

After going some eight leagues, toward evening they took one of the prisoners, to whom they made a harangue, enumerating the cruelties which he and his men had already practised toward them without any mercy, and that, in like manner, he ought to make up his mind to receive as much. They commanded him to sing, if he had courage, which he did; but it was a very sad song. [5]

MARQUETTE'S DISCOVERY OF THE MISSISSIPPI (1673)

MARQUETTE'S OWN ACCOUNT [1]

I embarked with M. Joliet, who had been chosen to conduct this enterprise, on the 13th May, 1673, with five other Frenchmen, in two bark canoes. We laid in some Indian corn and smoked beef for our voyage. We first took care, however, to draw from the Indians all the information we could, concerning the countries through which we designed to travel, and drew up a map, on which we marked down the rivers, nations, and points of the compass to guide us in our journey. The first nation we came to was called the Folles-Avoines, or the nation of wild oats. I entered their river to visit them, as I had preached among them some years before. The wild oats, from which they derive their name, grow spontaneously in their country....

I acquainted them with my design of discovering other nations, to preach to them the mysteries of our holy religion, at which they were much surprized, and said all they could to dissuade me from it. They told me I would meet Indians who spare no strangers, and whom they kill without any provocation or mercy; that the war they have one with the other would expose me to be taken by their warriors, as they are constantly on the look-out to surprize their enemies. That the Great River **[2]** was exceedingly dangerous, and full of frightful monsters who devoured men and canoes together, and that the heat was so great that it would positively cause our death. I thanked them for their kind advice, but told them I would not follow it, as the salvation of a great many souls was concerned in our undertaking, for whom I should be glad to lose my life, I added that I defied their monsters, and their information would oblige us to keep more upon our guard to avoid a surprize. And having prayed with them, and given them some instructions, we set out for the Bay of Puan, **[3]** where our missionaries had been successful in converting them.... The next day, being the 10th of June, the two guides [Miamies] embarked with us in sight of all the village, who were astonished at our attempting so dangerous an expedition. We were informed that at three leagues from the Maskoutens, we should find a river which runs into the Mississippi, and that we were to go to the west-south-west to find it, but there were so many marshes and lakes, that if it had not been for our guides we could not have found it....

Before embarking we all offered up prayers to the Holy Virgin, which we continued to do every morning, placing ourselves and the events of the journey under her protection, and after having encouraged each other, we got into our canoes. The river upon which we embarked is called Mesconsin [Wisconsin]; the river is very wide, but the sand bars make it very difficult to navigate, which is increased by numerous islands covered with grape-vines. The country through which it flows is beautiful; the groves are so dispersed in the prairies that it makes a noble prospect; and the fruit of the trees shows a fertile soil. These groves are full of walnut, oak, and other trees unknown to us in Europe. We saw neither game nor fish, but roebuck and buffaloes in great numbers. After having navigated thirty leagues we discovered some iron mines, and one of our company who had seen such mines before, said these were very rich in ore. They are covered with about three feet of soil, and situate near a chain of rocks, whose base is covered with fine timber. After having rowed ten leagues farther, making forty leagues from the place where we had embarked, we came into the Mississippi on the 17th of June [1673]. **[4]**

The mouth of the Mesconsin [Wisconsin] is in about 42½ N. lat. Behold us, then, upon this celebrated river, whose singularities I have attentively studied. The Mississippi takes its rise in several lakes in the North. Its channel is very narrow at the mouth of the Mesconsin, and runs south until it is affected by very high hills. Its current is slow, because of its depth. In sounding we found nineteen fathoms of water. A little further on it widens nearly three-quarters of a league, and the width continues to be more equal. We slowly followed its course to the south and southeast to the 42° N. lat. Here we perceived the country change its appearance. There were scarcely any more woods or mountains. The islands are covered with fine trees, but we could could not see any more roebucks, buffaloes, bustards, and swans. We met from time to time monstrous fish, which struck so violently against our canoes, that at first we took them to be large trees, which threatened to upset us. We saw also a hideous monster; his head was like that of a tiger, his nose was sharp, and somewhat resembled a wildcat; his beard was long; his ears stood upright; the color of his head was gray; and his neck black. He looked upon us for some time, but as we came near him our oars frightened him away. When we threw our nets into the water we caught an abundance of sturgeons, and another kind of fish like our trout, except that the eyes and nose are much smaller, and they have near the nose a bone like a woman's busk, three inches broad and a foot and a half long, the end of which is flat and broad, and when it leaps out of the water the weight of it throws it on its back.

Having descended the river as far as 41° 28', we found that turkeys took the place of game, and the Pisikious that of other animals. We called the Pisikious wild buffaloes, because they very much resemble our domestic oxen; they are not so long, but twice as large. We shot one of them, and it was as much as thirteen men could do to drag him from the place where he fell....

We continued to descend the river, not knowing where we were going, and having made an hundred leagues without seeing anything but wild beasts and birds, and being on our guard we landed at night to make our fire and prepare our repast, and then left the shore to anchor in the river, while one of us watched by turns to prevent a surprize. We went south and southwest until we found ourselves in about the latitude of 40° and some minutes, having rowed more than sixty leagues since we entered the river.

We took leave of our guides about the end of June, and embarked in presence of all the village, who admired our birch canoes, as they had never before seen anything like them. We descended the river, looking for another called Pekitanoni [Missouri], which runs from the northwest into the Mississippi....

As we were descending the river we saw high rocks with hideous monsters painted on them, and upon which the bravest Indians dare not look. They are as large as a calf, with head and horns like a goat; their eyes red; beard like a tiger's; and a face like a man's. Their tails are so long that they pass over their beads and between their fore legs, under their belly, and ending like a fish's tail. They are painted red, green, and black. They are so well drawn that I cannot believe they were drawn by the Indians. And for what purpose they were made seems to me a great mystery. As we fell down the river, and while we were discoursing upon these monsters, we heard a great rushing and bubbling of waters, and small islands of floating trees coming from the mouth of the Pekitanoni [Missouri], with such rapidity that we could not trust ourselves to go near it. The water of this river is so muddy that we could not drink it. It so discolors the Mississippi as to make the navigation of it dangerous. This river comes from the northwest, and empties into the Mississippi, and on its banks are situated a number of Indian villages. We judged by the compass, that the Mississippi discharged itself into the Gulf of Mexico. It would, however, have been more agreeable if it had discharged itself into the South Sea or Gulf of California....

Having satisfied ourselves that the Gulf of Mexico was in latitude 31° 40', and that we could reach it in three or four days' journey from the

Akansea [Arkansas River], and that the Mississippi discharged itself into it, and not to the eastward of the Cape of Florida, nor into the California Sea, we resolved to return home. We considered that the advantage of our travels would be altogether lost to our nation if we fell into the hands of the Spaniards, from whom we could expect no other treatment than death or slavery; besides, we saw that we were not prepared to resist the Indians, the allies of the Europeans, who continually infested the lower part of this river; we therefore came to the conclusion to return, and make a report to those who had sent us. So that having rested another day, we left the village of the Akansea, on the seventeenth of July, 1673, having followed the Mississippi from the latitude 42° to 34°, and preached the Gospel to the utmost of my power, to the nations we visited. We then ascended the Mississippi with great difficulty against the current, and left it in the latitude of 38° north, to enter another river [Illinois], which took us to the lake of the Illinois [Michigan], which is a much shorter way than through the River Mesconsin [Wisconsin], by which we entered the Mississippi....

THE DEATH OF MARQUETTE (1675)

BY FATHER CLAUDE DABLON [1]

Father James Marquette, having promised the Illinois, called Kaskaskia, to return among them to teach them our mysteries, had great difficulty in keeping his word. The great hardships of his first voyage had brought on a dysentery, and had so enfeebled him that he lost all hope of undertaking a second voyage. Yet, his malady having given way and almost ceased toward the close of summer in the following year, he obtained permission of his superiors to return to the Illinois to found that noble mission....

After the Illinois had taken leave of the father, filled with a great idea of the gospel, he continued his voyage, and soon after reached the Illinois Lake, on which he had nearly a hundred leagues to make by an unknown route, because he was obliged to take the southern [eastern] side of the lake, having gone thither by the northern [western]. His strength, however, failed so much that his men despaired of being able to carry him alive to their journey's end; for, in fact, he became so weak and exhausted that he could no longer help himself, nor even stir, and had to be handled and carried like a child....

The eve of his death, which was a Friday, he told them, all radiant with joy, that it would take place on the morrow. During the whole day he conversed with them about the manner of his burial, the way in which he should be laid out, the place to be selected for his interment; he told them how to arrange his hands, feet, and face, and directed them to raise a cross over his grave. He even went so far as to enjoin them, only three hours before he expired, to take his chapel-bell, as soon as he was dead, and ring it while they carried him to the grave. Of all this he spoke so calmly and collectedly that you would have thought that he spoke of the death and burial of another, and not of his own.

Thus did he speak with them as they sailed along the lake, till, perceiving the mouth of a river with an eminence on the bank which he thought suited for his burial, he told them that it was the place of his last repose. They wished, however, to pass on, as the weather permitted it and the day was not far advanced; but God raised a contrary wind which obliged them to return and enter the river pointed out by Father Marquette. They then carried him ashore, kindled a little fire, and raised for him a wretched bark cabin, where they laid him as little uncomfortably as they could; but they were so overcome by sadness that, as they afterward said, they did not know what they were doing.

The father being thus stretched on the shore, like Saint Francis Xavier, as he had always so ardently desired, and left alone amid those forests,—for his companions were engaged in unloading,—he had leisure to repeat all the acts in which he had been employed during the preceding days....

He had prayed his companions to remind him, when they saw him about to expire, to pronounce frequently the names of Jesus and Mary. When he could not do it himself, they did it for him; and, when they thought him about to pass, one cried aloud, Jesus Maria, which he several times repeated distinctly, and then, as if at those sacred names something had appeared to him, he suddenly raised his eyes above his crucifix, fixing them apparently on some object which he seemed to regard with pleasure, and thus with a countenance all radiant with smiles, he expired without a struggle, as gently as if he had sunk into a quiet sleep.

His two poor companions, after shedding many tears over his body, and having laid it out as he had directed, carried it devoutly to the grave, ringing the bell according to his injunction, and raised a large cross near it to serve as a mark for passers-by.

DISCOVERY OF NIAGARA FALLS (1678)

BY FATHER LOUIS HENNEPIN [1]

Betwixt the Lake Ontario and Erie, there is a vast and prodigious cadence of water which falls down after a surprizing and astonishing manner, insomuch that the universe does not afford its parallel. 'Tis true, Italy and Suedeland boast of some such things; but we may well say they are but sorry patterns, when compared to this of which we now speak. At the foot of this horrible precipice, we meet with the river Niagara, which is not above half a quarter of a league broad, but is wonderfully deep in some places. It is so rapid above this descent, that it violently hurries down the wild beasts while endeavoring to pass it to feed on the other side, they not being able to withstand the force of its current, which inevitably casts them down headlong above six hundred foot.

This wonderful downfall is compounded of two great cross-streams of water, and two falls, with an isle sloping along the middle of it. The waters which fall from this vast height, do foam and boil after the most hideous manner imaginable, making an outrageous noise, more terrible than that of thunder; for when the wind blows from off the south, their dismal roaring may be heard above fifteen leagues off.

The river Niagara having thrown itself down this incredible precipice, continues its impetuous course for two leagues together, to the great rock above mentioned, with an inexpressible rapidity: But having passed that, its impetuosity relents, gliding along more gently for two leagues, till it arrives at the Lake Ontario, or Frontenac.

Any bark or greater vessel may pass from the fort to the foot of this huge rock above mentioned. This rock lies to the westward, and is cut off from the land by the river Niagara, about two leagues farther down than the great fall; for which two leagues the people are obliged to carry their goods over-land; but the way is very good, and the trees are but few, and they chiefly firs and oaks.

From the great fall unto this rock, which is to the west of the river, the two brinks of it are so prodigious high, that it would make one tremble to look steadily upon the water, rolling along with a rapidity not to be imagined. Were it not for this vast cataract, which interrupts navigation, they might sail with barks or greater vessels, above four hundred and fifty leagues further, cross the Lake of Hurons, and up to the farther end of the Lake Illinois (Michigan); which two lakes we may well say are little seas of fresh water.

LA SALLE'S VOYAGE TO THE MOUTH OF THE MISSISSIPPI (1682)

BY FRANCIS PARKMAN [1]

La Salle chose eighteen of his Indian allies, whom he added to the twenty-three Frenchmen who remained with him, some of the rest having deserted, and others lagged behind. The Indians insisted on taking their squaws with them. These were ten in number, besides three children; and thus the expedition included fifty-four persons, of whom some were useless, and others a burden.

On the 21st of December, Tonty and Membré set out from Fort Miami with some of the party in six canoes, and crossed to the little river Chicago. La Salle, with the rest of the men, joined them a few days later. It was the dead of winter, and the streams were frozen. They made sledges, placed on them the canoes, the baggage, and a disabled Frenchman; crossed from the Chicago to the northern branch of the Illinois, and filed in a long procession down its frozen course. They reached the site of the great Illinois village, found it tenantless, and continued their journey, still dragging their canoes, till at length they reached open water below Lake Peoria.

La Salle had abandoned for a time his original plan of building a vessel for the navigation of the Mississippi. Bitter experience [2] had taught him the difficulty of the attempt, and he resolved to trust to his canoes alone. They embarked again, floating prosperously down between the leafless forests that flanked the tranquil river; till, on the sixth of February, they issued upon the majestic bosom of the Mississippi. Here, for the time, their progress was stopt; for the river was full of floating ice. La Salle's Indians, too, had lagged behind; but, within a week, all had arrived, the navigation was once more free, and they resumed their course. Toward evening, they saw on their right the mouth of a great river; and the clear current was invaded by the headlong torrent of the Missouri, opaque with mud. They built their camp-fires in the neighboring forests; and at daylight, embarking anew on the dark and mighty stream, drifted swiftly down toward unknown destinies. They passed a deserted town of the Tamaroas; saw, three days after, the mouth of the Ohio; and, gliding by the wastes of bordering swamp, landed on the twenty-fourth of February near the Third Chickasaw Bluffs. They encamped, and the hunters went out for game. All returned, excepting Pierre Prudhomme; and, as the others had seen fresh tracks of Indians, La Salle feared that he was killed. While some of his followers built a small stockade fort on a high bluff by the river, others ranged the woods in pursuit of the missing hunter. After six days of ceaseless and fruitless search, they met two Chickasaw Indians in the forest; and, through them, La Salle sent presents and peace-messages to that warlike people, whose villages were a few days' journey distant. Several days later, Prudhomme was found, and brought in to the camp, half-dead. He had lost his way while hunting; and, to console him for his woes, La Salle christened the newly-built fort with his name, and left him, with a few others, in charge of it.

Again they embarked; and, with every stage of their adventurous progress, the mystery of this vast New World was more and more unveiled. More and more they entered the realms of spring. The hazy sunlight, the warm and drowsy air, the tender foliage, the opening flowers, betokened the reviving life of Nature. For several days more they followed the writhings of the great river, on its tortuous course through wastes of swamp and canebrake, till on the thirteenth of March they found themselves wrapt in a thick fog. Neither shore was visible; but they heard on the right the booming of an Indian drum and the shrill outcries of the war-dance. La Salle at once crossed to the opposite side, where, in less than an hour, his men threw up a rude fort of felled trees. Meanwhile, the fog cleared; and, from the farther bank, the astonished Indians saw the strange visitors at their work. Some of the French advanced to the edge of the water, and beckoned them to come over. Several of them approached, in a wooden canoe, to within the distance of a gun-shot. La Salle displayed the calumet, and sent a Frenchman to meet them. He was well received; and, the friendly mood of the Indians being now apparent, the whole party crossed the river.

On landing, they found themselves at a town of the Kappa band of the Arkansas, a people dwelling near the mouth of the river which bears their name. "The whole village," writes Membré to his superior, "came down to the shore to meet us, except the women, who had run off. I cannot tell you the civility and kindness we received from these barbarians, who brought us poles to make huts, supplied us with firewood during the three days we were among them, and took turns in feasting us. We did not lose the value of a pin while we were among them." ...

After touching at several other towns of this people, the voyagers resumed their course, guided by two of the Arkansas; passed the sites, since become historic, of Vicksburg and Grand Gulf; and, about three hundred miles below the Arkansas, stopt by the edge of a swamp on the western side of the river. Here, as their two guides told them, was the path to the great town of the Taensas. Tonty and Membré were sent to visit it. They and their men shouldered their birch canoe through the swamp, and launched it on a lake which had once formed a portion of the channel of the river.

In two hours they reached the town; and Tonty gazed at it with astonishment. He had seen nothing like it in America: large square dwellings, built of sun-baked mud mixed with straw, arched over with a dome-shaped roof of canes, and placed in regular order around an open area. Two of them were larger and better than the rest. One was the lodge of the chief; the other was the temple, or house of the sun. They entered the former, and found a single room, forty feet square, where, in the dim light, — for there was no opening but the door, — the chief sat awaiting them on a sort of bedstead, three of his wives at his side, while sixty old men, wrapt in white cloaks woven of mulberry-bark, formed his divan. When he spoke, his wives howled to do him honor; and the assembled councilors listened with the reverence due to a potentate for whom, at his death, a hundred victims were to be sacrificed. He received the visitors graciously, and joyfully accepted the gifts which Tonty laid before him. This interview over, the Frenchmen repaired to the temple, wherein were kept the bones of the departed chiefs. In construction, it was much like the royal dwelling. Over it were rude wooden figures, representing three eagles turned toward the east. A strong mud wall surrounded it, planted with stakes, on which were stuck the skulls of enemies sacrificed to the Sun; while before the door was a block of wood, on which lay a large shell surrounded with the braided hair of the victims. The interior was rude as a barn, dimly lighted from the doorway, and full of smoke. There was a structure in the middle which Membré thinks was a kind of altar; and before it burned a perpetual fire, fed with three logs laid end to end, and watched by two old men devoted to this sacred office. There was a mysterious recess, too, which the strangers were forbidden to explore, but which, as Tonty was told, contained the riches of the nation, consisting of pearls from the Gulf, and trinkets obtained, probably through other tribes, from the Spaniards and other Europeans....

On the next morning, as they descended the river, they saw a wooden canoe full of Indians; and Tonty gave chase. He had nearly overtaken it, when more than a hundred men appeared suddenly on the shore, with bows bent to defend their countrymen. La Salle called out to Tonty to withdraw. He obeyed; and the whole party encamped on the opposite bank. Tonty offered to cross the river with a peace-pipe, and set out accordingly with a small party of men. When he landed, the Indians made signs of friendship by joining their hands,—a proceeding by which Tonty, having but one hand, was somewhat embarrassed [3] ; but he directed his men to respond in his stead.

The Indians of this village were the Natchez; and their chief was brother of the great chief, or Sun, of the whole nation. His town was several leagues distant, near the site of the city of Natchez; and thither the French repaired to visit him. They saw what they had already seen among the Taensas,—a religious and political despotism, a privileged caste descended from the sun, a temple, and a sacred fire. La Salle planted a large cross, with the arms of France attached, in the midst of the town; while the inhabitants looked on with a satisfaction which they would hardly have displayed, had they understood the meaning of the act....

And now they neared their journey's end. On the sixth of April, the river divided itself into three broad channels. La Salle followed that of the west, and D'Autray that of the east; while Tonty took the middle passage. As he drifted down the turbid current, between the low and marshy shores, the brackish water changed to brine, and the breeze grew fresh with the salt breath of the sea. Then the broad bosom of the great Gulf opened on his sight, tossing its restless billows, limitless, voiceless, lonely as when born of chaos, without a sail, without a sign of life.

La Salle, in a canoe, coasted the marshy borders of the sea; and then the reunited parties assembled on a spot of dry ground, a short distance above the mouth of the river. Here a column was made ready, bearing the arms of France, and inscribed with the words,—"LOUIS LE GRAND, ROY DE FRANCE ET DE NAVARRE, REGNE; LE NEUVIEME 1682." ...

On that day, the realm of France received on parchment a stupendous accession. The fertile plains of Texas; the vast basin of the Mississippi, from its frozen northern springs to the sultry borders of the Gulf; from the woody ridges of the Alleghanies to the bare peaks of the Rocky Mountains,—a region of savannas and forests, sun-cracked deserts, and grassy prairies, watered by a thousand rivers, ranged by a thousand warlike tribes, passed beneath the scepter of the Sultan of Versailles; and all by virtue of a feeble human voice, inaudible at half a mile.

FOOTNOTES

THE MEN FROM ASIA AND FROM NORWAY

[1] From an article by Mr. Winsor in "The Narrative and Critical History of America," of which he was editor. By arrangement with the publishers, Houghton, Mifflin Co., Copyright 1889. For a long period Mr. Winsor was librarian of Harvard University. He wrote "From Cartier to Frontenac," "Christopher Columbus," "The Mississippi Basin," and made other important contributions to American history.

HOW THE NORWEGIANS CAME TO VINLAND

[1] From "The Saga of Eric the Red," as given in the "Old South Leaflets." Two different versions of this saga exist, the first written by Hauk Erlendsson between 1305 and 1334; the second by Jon Thordharson, about 1387. Both are believed to have been based on writings that had come down from the time of the explorations.

Confirmation of the truth of the Norwegian discovery is given in a book by Adam of Bremen, who visited Denmark between 1047 and 1073, and makes reference to Norwegian colonies founded in Iceland and Greenland and in another country which was "called Vinland on account of the wild grapes that grow there." Mention is also made by this writer of corn as growing in Vinland without cultivation. He declares his statements to be based on "trustworthy reports of the Danes." John Fiske thought Vinland lay somewhere between Point Judith and Cape Breton.

THE FIRST CHILD OF EUROPEAN RACE BORN IN AMERICA

[1] From the "Saga"' of Hauk Erlendsson. Except for the Norse discovery, the honor of being the first child of Anglo-Saxon race born in America would belong to Virginia Dare. Virginia Dare was born in Virginia during one of the attempted settlements under Sir Walter Raleigh. An account of her is given in Volume II of this work. Children of Spanish and French parents had, of course, been born in America before the date of Virginia Dare's birth.

[2] By Skrellings the author means natives.

OTHER PRE-COLUMBIAN VOYAGES

[1] From Mr. Wheaton's "History of the Northmen," published in 1831. Mr. Wheaton was a native of Providence, R.I., and died in Roxbury, Mass., in 1848, at the age of 63. He was an eminent lawyer and publicist and author of "Elements of International Law," a legal classic.

AS DESCRIBED BY WASHINGTON IRVING

[1] From Irving's "Life of Columbus." By permission of the publishers, G.P. Putnam's Sons.

AS DESCRIBED BY COLUMBUS HIMSELF

[1] The first letter of Columbus, descriptive of his first voyage, was written in February, 1498, when he was off the Azores, on his return home. It was addrest to Louis de Santangel, the treasurer of King Ferdinand of Spain. Altho addrest to the treasurer, it was intended for the eyes of the King himself, and for those of his queen, Isabella. The letter was first printed in Barcelona, soon after the arrival of Columbus. Another account, substantially the same, was written by Columbus in Lisbon in March of the same year, an—at once translated into Latin and published in Rome in several editions, one being that of Stephen Plannck, of which five copies only are now known to be extant. Of this Plannck edition a translation from the Latin into English made by Henry W. Haynes has been published by the New York Public Library. From this translation the passage here given is taken.

[2] The identity of the island on which Columbus made his first landing was formerly much in controversy. The best opinion now inclines to accept the conclusions reached by Captain Beecher of the British Navy some fifty years ago, that the landing was made on what is known as Watling's Island, one of the Bahamas. This island is about thirteen miles long, north and south, and six wide, and is made up of coral, shell and other marine debris. A monument was erected on it by a Chicago newspaper in 1892, with this inscription: "On this spot Christopher Columbus first set foot on the soil of the New World." The monument is said already to be in a state of decay, having been poorly constructed. Watling's Island lies about 200 miles southeast of Nassau, and is nearly on a parallel with Havana, but lies 400 miles east of it. Its inhabitants number about 700, who are dispersed among fifteen hamlets. The horses on the island scarcely number 50. There

are a few cows and several flocks of sheep. The people are all poor. Little is grown on the island, droughts occur, and starvation has in some years been prevented only by help from outside.

THE BULL OF POPE ALEXANDER VI. PARTITIONING AMERICA

[1] Dated at Rome, May 4th, 1498. It was translated into English by Richard Eden in 1555, and is printed in Old English and from black-letter type, by Hart in his "American History Told by Contemporaries." For the present work the English has been modernized.

This famous bull was the result of rival claims, made by Spain and Portugal, to lands discovered beyond the Atlantic. More than half a century before Columbus found America, the Portuguese had secured from Pope Eugenius IV a grant in perpetuity of all heathen lands that might be discovered by them in further voyages. The grant went so far as to include "the Indies," and was confirmed by succeeding popes.

When Alexander VI issued his bull the America which Columbus had found was believed to be not a new continent, but the Indies, and the Portuguese, who had reached India by way of the Cape of Good Hope, were threatening to send an expedition across the Atlantic to take possession and dispute the Spanish claims. It was in these circumstances, and for the purpose of reconciling the rival states that Alexander issued the bull, John Fiske has said that, "As between the two rival powers the Pontiff's arrangement was made in a spirit of even-handed justice." The bull conferred on the Spanish sovereigns all the lands already discovered, or thereafter to be discovered in the western ocean, with jurisdiction and privileges In all respects similar to those formerly bestowed upon the crown of Portugal.

Alexander VI, the famous Borgia Pope, who was the father of Caesar Borgia and Lucretia Borgia, has been accused, somewhat loosely, of committing an act of foolish audacity in making this grant. He has been represented as having partitioned the whole American continent between Spain and Portugal. The accusation is quite unjust. The bull merely granted such lands as had been discovered, or might yet be discovered, and these lands were not understood to be those of a new continent, but parts of India not heretofore explored. As for any rights possess by other European countries, including England and France, those countries at that time had little, if any, interest in the discovery made by Columbus or, in fact, any actual knowledge of it.

THE DISCOVERY OF THE MAINLAND BY THE CABOTS—
THE ACCOUNT GIVEN BY JOHN A. DOYLE

[1] From Doyle's "English Colonies in America." Published by Henry Holt & Co. The Cabots in 1497 discovered what came to be known afterward as the continent of North America, Columbus in 1492 having discovered only islands in the West Indies. The work of the Cabots in after years was a basis of English claims to the continent because of priority of discovery. It was not until his third expedition, fourteen months after the discovery made by the Cabots, that Columbus first saw the North American mainland.

THE DISCOVERY OF THE MAINLAND BY THE CABOTS—
PETER MARTYR'S ACCOUNT

[1] Peter Martyr, a native of Milan, resided for some years at the Spanish court. The account he gives in this article of the voyage of the Cabots is based on information received by him directly from Sabastian Cabot, when Cabot was employed as pilot in the service of Spain. Martyr's account is the earliest complete narrative of this voyage now extant. It therefore takes high rank—in fact, is the corner-stone—among documents pertaining to steps by which English civilization became supreme in North America. The translation here given, made by Richard Eden, was published in London in 1555.

THE VOYAGES OF VESPUCIUS

[1] Americus Vespucius was born in Florence in 1452 and died in Seville in 1512. He was the son of a notary in Florence, was educated by a Dominican friar and became a clerk in one of the commercial houses of the Medici. By this house he was sent to Spain in 1490. He remained some years in Seville, where he became connected with the house which fitted out the second expedition of Columbus.

Vespucius claimed to have been four times in America, first in May, 1497; second, in May, 1499; third, in May, 1501; fourth, in June, 1503. In writing of the first expedition he says his ship reached a coast "which we thought to be that of the continent," giving date. If this assumption be correct, and the dates correct, they would show that he reached the continent of North America a week or two before the Cabots made their discovery farther north, but this contention has never been satisfactorily supported.

The letters of Vespucius describing his four voyages were published originally in Italian in Florence in 1505-6. The letter here in part given was addrest by Vespucius to Soderini, the Gonfalonier of Florence. The translation, by one "M.K.," was published by Mr. Quaritch, the London bookseller, in 1885, and has been printed as one of the "Old South Leaflets!" The letter is believed to have been composed by Vespucius within a month after his return from his second voyage.

Vespucius was a naval astronomer. He has been unjustly accused of appropriating to himself an honor which belonged to Columbus,—that of giving a name to the new continent. This injustice, however, was not due to Vespucius, but to a German schoolmaster named Hylacomylus, or "Miller of the Wood-pond," who published a book in 1507. The passage in Millers book in which he made a suggestion which the world has adopted is as follows:

"And the fourth part of the world having been discovered by Americus, it may be called Amerige; that is, the land of Americus, or America. Now, truly sience these regions are more widely explored, and another fourth part is discovered by Americus Vespucius, I do not see why any one may justly forbid it to be named Amerige; that is, Americ's Land, after Americus, the discoverer, who is a man of sagacious mind; or call it America, since both Europe and Asia derived their names from women."

Vespucius, in spite of several voyages, discovered very little in America. The continent ought not to have been named alter him.

A BATTLE WITH THE INDIANS

[1] From a letter addrest by Vespucius to Pier Soderini, Gonfalonier of Florence. A translation is printed in the "Old South Leaflets." Vespucius, during one of his voyages, is believed to have discovered the coast of South America—perhaps as far down as the mouth of La Plata. His letters, however, give slight clue to localities. Few of the places described by him have ever been identified with anything like precision.

THE FIRST ACCOUNT OF AMERICA PRINTED IN ENGLISH

[1] The volume from which this passage is taken was first printed in Antwerp as a compilation with additions based on the letters of Americus Vespucius. It is included by Edward Arber in his "First Three English Books on America." The author's name is unknown.

THE DISCOVERY OF FLORIDA BY PONCE DE LEON

[1] From Parkman's "Pioneers of France in the New World." By permission of the publishers, Little, Brown & Co. Ponce do Leon was born in Aragon, Spain, about 1460, and died in Cuba in 1521. Before making the exploration here described, he had been in America with Columbus in 1493; been governor of the eastern part of Espanola; been transferred to Porto Rico as governor, and empowered to conquer the Indians. He returned to Spain in 1511 and in February, 1512, was commissioned to discover and settle the island of Bimini. This island, one of the Bahamas, was in the region in which tradition had placed the Fountain of Youth. After his expedition to Florida here described, he was occupied with Indian wars in Porto Rico and Florida, and finally died from a wound received from an arrow shot by an Indian.

[2] Parkman comments on this tradition of the Fountain of Youth as follows: "The story has an explanation, sufficiently characteristic, having been suggested, it is said, by the beauty of the native women, which none could resist and which kindled the fires of youth in the veins of age."

THE DISCOVERY OF THE PACIFIC BY BALBOA

[1] Quintand's account of this expedition is the best we have in Spanish literature. It forms part of his "Lives of Celebrated Spaniards" (1807-1833), a standard work of the encyclopedia class. Vasco Nunez de Balboa was born at Xerxes, in Spain, in 1475, and died in Panama about 1517. His first visit to America was made in 1500. Ten years later he went to Darien, where he became alcalde of a new settlement. In 1512 he was made governor of San Domingo.

While Governor of San Domingo Balboa learned from the Indians that there was a great sea lying to the south and west, and in September, 1513, set out from Darien to discover it. After an adventurous journey he reached, on September 25th, a mountain top from which he first saw the Pacific. After building some ships for use on the Pacific and transporting them with immense labor across the Isthmus, launching two of them, Balboa was arrested by the governor of the colony on a charge of contemplated revolt and beheaded.

[2] Careta was an Indian chief whose friendship Balboa secured.

[3] The date of this view of the Pacific by Balboa was September 25, 1513. Readers of the poems of Keats are familiar with the error in his sonnet

"On First Looking Into Chapman's 'Homer,'" where, by a curious error, never corrected, he makes Cortez, instead of Balboa, the Spaniard who stood "silent upon a peak in Darien."

THE VOYAGE OF MAGELLAN TO THE PACIFIC

[1] From Fiske's "Discovery of America." Copyright, 1892, by John Fiske. Reprinted by arrangement with the publishers, Houghton, Mifflin Co. Ferdinand Magellan was born at Saborosa in Portugal, about 1480, and died in the Philippines in 1521. Before discovering the strait that bears his name he had served with the Portuguese in the East Indies and in Morocco. Becoming dissatisfied he had gone to Spain, where he proposed to find a western passage to the Moluccas, a proposal which Charles V accepted, fitting out for him a government squadron of five ships and 265 men. Magellan sailed from San Lucar September 20, 1519, and, after passing through the strait as here described by Fiske, proceeded to the Philippines, where, in an attack on unfriendly natives, he, with several of his men, was killed. One of his ships afterward completed the voyage by way of the Cape of Good Hope, and thus made the first circumnavigation of the globe.

[2] A reference to Sir Francis Drake, the first Englishman who circumnavigated the globe.

THE DISCOVERY OF NEW YORK HARBOR BY VERAZZANO

[1] From a letter addrest to Francis I, King of France, on July 8, 1524. Three copies of Verazzano's letter exist. One was printed by Ramusio in 1556 and translated for Hakluyt's "Voyages" in 1583. The second was found in the Strozzi Library in Florence, and published in 1841 by the New York Historical Society with a translation by J.G. Cogswell.

The third copy is the one now owned by Count Gulio Macchi di Cellere, of Rome. It was first published in Italy in 1909, and the first English translation of it was made by Dr. Edward Hagaman Hall, secretary of the American Scenic and Historic Preservation Society, and published in the report of that society for 1910. This copy has the distinction of being contemporaneous. Dr. Hall says its value "consists not only in confirming the voyage itself, but also in supplying a wealth of names and details not previously known to exist." Verazzano's account of his visit to New York harbor here given is taken from Dr. Hall's translation.

Giovanni de Verazzano was born in Italy about 1480, and died about 1527. He early became a Florentine navigator and afterward a corsair in

French service. His expedition to America was of French origin and sailed in 1523.

[2] Off the coast of Virginia or Maryland.

[3] This river is now known as the Hudson.

[4] Verazzano's Bay, St. Margarita, was New York Bay.

[5] Aloysia is now called Block Island.

[6] Newport.

[7] Cape Cod.

[8] A Reference to the discovery of Newfoundland in 1497.

CARTIER'S EXPLORATION OF THE ST. LAWRENCE—THE ACCOUNT GIVEN BY JOHN A. DOYLE

[1] From Doyle's *"English Colonies in America."* By permission of the publishers, Henry Holt & Co. Jacques Cartier was born at St. Malo, France, in 1494, and died some time after 1552. He made three voyages to Canada, the first in 1534, the second in 1535, the third in 1541.

[2] The site is now occupied by Montreal.

CARTIER'S EXPLORATION OF THE ST. LAWRENCE—CARTIER'S OWN ACCOUNT

[1] From a letter by Cartier, of which a translation exists in Hakluyt's "Principal Navigations," etc. Printed in Hart's "American History Told by Contemporaries."

[2] The Gulf of St. Lawrence.

SEARCHES FOR "THE SEVEN CITIES OF CIBOLA"

[1] From Mr. Thwaites' "Rocky Mountain Explorations." By permission of the publishers, D. Appleton & Co. Copyright 1904. Cabeza de Vaca was born at Jeraz de la Frontera, in Spain, about 1490, and died at Seville some time after 1560. In 1528 he was made treasurer of an expedition under Narvaez to Florida. From Florida he sailed westward with Narvaez and off the coast of Lousiana was shipwrecked. A combat with Indians ensued from

which De Vaca and three others escaped with their lives. After spending six years with the Indians as captives, he reached Mexico in 1536, meanwhile making the journey here described. He returned to Spain in 1537, and in 1540 was made Governor of Paraguay, which he explored in 1543. In the following year he was deposed and imprisoned by Spanish colonists in Paraguay for alleged arbitrary conduct and sent to Spain, where he was sentenced to be banished to Oran in Africa, but was subsequently recalled and made judge of the Supreme Court of Seville.

CABEZA DE VACA'S JOURNEY TO THE SOUTHWEST

[1] After returning to Spain De Vaca published at Zemora, in 1542, a "Relation" of his travels and adventures, from which the account here given is taken. Purchase issued an early English version of it, but a better translation, made in 1851 by Buckingham Smith, is printed in the "Old South Leaflets." The passages here given relate to the journey through Texas, Oklahoma, New Mexico, and Arizona. The exact localities, however, it has been impossible to identify.

[2] Not the domestic cow we know, which was brought to America from Europe, but the cow of the bison, or buffalo.

THE EXPEDITION OF CORONADO TO THE SOUTHWEST

[1] From Coronado's letter to Mendoza, dated August 3, 1540, Mendoza being Viceroy of Mexico, by whom Coronado had been sent out. Coronado's expedition was a great disappointment to all concerned in it, inasmuch as it resulted in failure to find the fabled "seven cities of Cibola." He had 300 Spaniards with him and 800 Indians. Instead of finding great towns, as promised by Marcos and others, he discovered only a poor village of 200 people, situated on a rocky eminence. The expedition, however, in spite of this failure, remains one of the most important exploring expeditions ever undertaken in America. Opinions differ as to how far north Coronado went, some maintaining that he reached a point north of the boundary line between Kansas and Nebraska. His letter was printed by Hakluyt in Volume III of his "Voyages," and may be found in the "Old South Leaflets." Mr. Thwaites says of the expedition:

> "Disappointed, but still hoping to find the country of
> gold, Coronado's gallant little army, frequently thinned
> by death and desertion, for three years beat up and down

the southwestern wilderness: now thirsting in the deserts, now penned up in gloomy canons, now crawling over pathless mountains, suffering the horrors of starvation and of despair, but following this will-o'-the-wisp with a melancholy perseverance seldom seen in man save when searching for some mysterious treasure. Coronado apparently twice crossed the State of Kansas. 'Through mighty plains and sandy heaths,' says the chronicler of the expedition, 'smooth and wearisome and bare of wood. All that way the plains are as full of crookback oxen (buffaloes) as the mountain Serena in Spain is of sheep. They were a great succor for the hunger and want of bread which our people stood in. One day it rained in that plain a great shower of hail as big as oranges, which caused many tears, weaknesses, and vows.' The wanderer ventured as far as the Missouri, and would have gone still farther eastward but for his inability to cross the swollen river. Cooperating parties explored the upper valleys of the Rio Grande and Gila, ascended the Colorado for two hundred and forty miles above its mouth, and visited the Grand Canon of the same river. Coronado at last returned, satisfied that he had been victimized by the idle tales of travelers. He was rewarded with contumely and lost his place as governor of New Galicia; but his romantic march stands in history as one of the most remarkable exploring expeditions of modern times."

Francisco Vasquez de Coronado was born at Salamanca, in Spain, about 1500, and died in Mexico some time after 1542. He is believed to have gone to Mexico in 1535 with Mendoza, the viceroy, who, in 1539, made him governor of a province.

[2] Marcos is here referred to.

THE DISCOVERY OF THE MISSISSIPPI BY DE SOTO

[1] From Parkman's "Pioneers of France in the New World." By permission of the publishers, Little, Brown & Co. Hernando de Soto was born in Badaios, Spain, in 1500, and died near the Mississippi River, probably on May 21, 1542. Before discovering the Mississippi, he had been

in Panama and Nicaragua; had been active with Pizarro in the conquest of Peru, from which he returned very rich to Spain, and in 1587 had been appointed Governor of Cuba and Florida, with orders to explore and settle the country. It was while engaged in the latter work that he discovered the Mississippi.

De Soto's route has been determined only approximately. He is believed first to have made a circuit northward from Tampa, through Florida into Georgia and perhaps into Carolina, thence going westward to Alabama and Mobile Bay. From the latter he turned northward again, thence going westward to the Mississippi, which he is believed to have crossed at Chickasaw Bluffs, in May, 1541. From this point he went northward and almost reached the Missouri. He then turned southward, and reached the junction of the Red River and Mississippi, where he died of malaria fever. Of his men 250 perished from disease or in combat with the Indians.

[2] The bison, or buffalo, is here referred to.

THE DEATH OF DE SOTO

[1] From the "Narrative of the Gentleman of Elvas," the author's name being unknown, but written by one of De Soto's companions, a Spaniard, and first printed in 1557. The author has been supposed to be Alvaro Fernandez, but this is only a matter of conjecture. The translation here used is that made by Hakluyt, printed in London in 1809, and included in the "Old South Leaflets."

DRAKE'S VISIT TO CALIFORNIA

[1] From "The World Encompassed by Sir Francis Drake," the author's name unknown. This work was prepared from notes made by Francis Fletcher, the chaplain of Drake's ship and by "divers others of his followers in the same," under the direction of Drake's heir and nephew, and was published in London in 1628 "both for the honor of the actor, but especially for the starting up of heroic spirits to benefit their country and eternize their own names by like noble attempts."

It has been contended that Drake fully believed that by his discoveries in America he had laid the foundations of an English civilization here, as a rival to Spanish civilizations. Spain then had a practical monopoly of settlements in America. It is to be remembered that Drake's work was in advance of all the English settlements and attempts at settlements on the Atlantic coast, including those of Gosnold, Amidas and Barlow, Sir Humphrey Gilbert and Raleigh. Drake named the country he had visited Albion. He may have gone as far north as Vancouver. There seems to be no doubt that he reached the Bay of San Francisco, and perhaps repaired his ships there.

Drake was born in Tavistock, in England, about 1540, and died off Porto Bello in 1596. Before making his visit to the Pacific coast he had served under Sir John Hawkins, as commander of a small vessel, which went out against the Spanish; had visited the West Indies and commanded a freebooting expedition in which he captured an immense treasure, afterward abandoned; had burned a Spanish vessel at Cartagena, and captured several ships; had crossed the Isthmus of Panama and become the first Englishman to see the Pacific, and had served in Ireland under the Earl of Essex.

It was in December, 1577, that he started on the expedition during which he visited the Pacific coast as here described. It was a freebooting enterprise. Drake sailed through the Strait of Magellan. After visiting California he crossed the Pacific, and, reaching England by way of the Cape of Good Hope in 1580, Drake became the first Englishman to circumnavigate the globe. Queen Elizabeth on his return knighted him on board his own ship. His after career was equally notable, including as it did an important command under Lord Howard in the great sea fight of July, 1588, in which the Armada of Spain was overthrown In the English Channel.

HUDSON'S DISCOVERY OF THE HUDSON RIVER

[1] Juet, on a previous voyage with Hudson, had been Hudson's mate, but on the voyage to New York Harbor he was his clerk and kept a journal. From this document, which is included in the "Old South Leaflets," the account here given is taken. Hudson himself also kept a journal, but this has been lost. It is curious that Juet, on the last voyage which Hudson made— the one to Hudson Bay, in which he was sent adrift in a small boat and left to perish—became the leader in the mutiny.

Before coming to America, Henry Hudson, an Englishman in Dutch service, had sailed to the east coast of Greenland, visited Spitzbergen, and attempted to find a northeast passage from the Atlantic to the Pacific. It was his attempt to find a northwest passage which led him, in September, 1609, into the harbor of New York and up the river named after him. In the following year he sailed again from Holland, seeking a northwest passage and thus entered Hudson Bay. Here he spent the winter. In the following June, when about to return home, the crew mutinied; Hudson, and eight others, were seized, bound and set afloat in a small boat that was never heard from again.

[2] Sandy Hook.

[3] Probably Staten Island.

[4] Coney Island.

[5] The Narrows.

[6] Moulton, in his "History of New York," inclines to the view that this point was near what is now known as Manhattanville in New York City.

[7] This was in the neighborhood of Stony Point.

[8] The Catskill Mountains.

[9] The neighborhood of Albany.

[10] Moulton's view is that this encounter took place near Fort Washington, New York City.

CHAMPLAIN'S BATTLE WITH THE IROQUOIS ON LAKE CHAMPLAIN

[1] From the "Voyages of Samuel de Champlain," as published by the Prince Society of Boston in 1878, the translation being by Charles Pomeroy Otis.

Samuel de Champlain, who has been called "The Father of New France," was born in Brouage, France, in 1567, and died in Quebec in 1635. Parkman accepts this title as just, and adds that in Champlain were embodied the religious zeal of New France and her romantic spirit of adventure. Champlain's first explorations in America were made in 1603-07. Quebec was founded by him in 1608, and Lake Champlain discovered in 1609.

[2] Now called the Richelieu River.

[3] Lake Champlain.

[4] The Adirondacks or the Green Mountains might have been here referred to.

[5] Parkman, in his "Pioneers of France in the New World," adds to this narrative the following: "At night the victors led out one of the prisoners, told him that he was to die by fire, and ordered him to sing his death-song, if he dared. Then they began the torture, and presently scalped their victim alive, when Champlain, sickening at the sight, begged leave to shoot him. They refused, and he turned away in anger and disgust; on which they called him back and told him to do as he pleased. He turned again and a shot from his arquebuse put the wretch out of misery. The scene filled him with horror; but, a few months later, on the Place de la Grave, at Paris, he might have witnessed tortures equally revolting and equally vindictive, inflicted on the regicide Ravaillac by the sentence of grave and learned judges. [Ravaillac was the assassin of Henry IV.]

"The allies made a prompt retreat from the scene of their triumph. Three or four days brought them to the mouth of the Richelieu. Here they separated; the Hurons and Algonquins made for the Ottawa, their homeward route, each with a share of prisoners for future torments. At parting they invited Champlain to visit their towns, and aid them again in their wars, an invitation which the paladin of the woods failed not to accept.

"The companions now remaining to him were the Montagnais. In their camp on the Richelieu, one of them dreamed that a war party of Iroquois was close upon them; on which, in a torrent of rain, they left their huts, paddled in dismay to the islands above the Lake of St. Peter, and hid themselves all night in the rushes. In the morning they took heart, emerged from their hiding-places, descended to Quebec, and went thence to Tadousac, whither Champlain accompanied them. Here the squaws, stark naked, swam out to the canoes to receive the heads of the dead Iroquois, and, hanging them from their necks, danced in triumph along the shore. One of the heads and a pair of arms were then bestowed on Champiain,—touching memorials of gratitude, which, however, he was by no means to keep for himself, but to present to the King.

"Thus did New France rush into collision with the redoubted warriors of the Five Nations. Here was the beginning, and in some measure doubtless the cause, of a long suite of murderous conflicts, bearing havoc and flame to generations yet unborn. Champlain had invaded the tiger's den; and now, in smothered fury, the patient savage would lie biding his day of blood."

MARQUETTE'S DISCOVERY OF THE MISSISSIPPI

[1] Father Marquette was born at Laon, in France, in 1637, and died on the eastern shore of Lake Michigan in 1675. Marquette had kept daily memoranda of his expedition, but during the return voyage up the Mississippi his papers were lost. He afterward composed from memory his narrative published under the title "Travels and Discoveries in North America." It has been printed in the "Historical Collections of Louisiana," and in Hart's "American History Told by Contemporaries."

In this journey, occupying about four months, Marquette and Joliet paddled their canoes more than 2,500 miles. It has been maintained by some writers, and among them Mr. Thwaites, that Joliet and Marquette were as much the real discoverers of the Mississippi as Columbus was the discoverer of America. While Europeans had actually reached the Mississippi before them, just as Asiatics and Norwegians probably had reached America before Columbus, it was Joliet and Marquette who first wrote narratives of their expedition, prepared excellent maps, and were followed by others who opened the region to enterprise and settlement. Of de Soto's century-and-a-quarter earlier discovery, nothing came, while the contention put forth for La Salle that he made an earlier visit than Joliet and Marquette is based "on the merest surmise."

[2] The Mississippi.

[3] The arm of Lake Michigan, now called Green Bay.

[4] The town of Prairie du Chien lies just north of the confluence of the Wisconsin and Mississippi rivers.

THE DEATH OF MARQUETTE

[1] From Dablon's "Relation." Dablon was the Superior General of the Jesuit Missions in America.

DISCOVERY OF NIAGARA FALLS

[1] Louis Hennepin, born in Belgium in 1640, was a friar of the Recollect order, an offshoot of the Franciscans. Mr. Thwaites, who has edited Hennepin's "New Discovery of a Vast Country," from which the account of Niagara Falls here given is taken, describes him as "an uneasy soul, uncontent to remain cloistered and fretting to engage in travel and wild adventure." After the pioneer voyage down the Mississippi, made by Joliet and Marquette, had become known in Europe, it intensified an already active spirit of discovery. In the summer of 1678 Hennepin joined La Salle and Laval Montmorency in the famous expedition of La Salle undertaken from Quebec to explore the interior, with a view to uniting Canada with the Gulf of Mexico by a chain of forts. On arrival in Quebec Father Hennepin was sent forward by La Salle to Fort Frontenac, on Lake Ontario. Thence, with La Monte and sixteen men, he went on to Niagara in order to smooth the way with the Indians for La Salle's later coming. It was at this time that Hennepin first saw Niagara Falls. White men had probably seen the cataract before, but he is the first who wrote a description of it that has come down to us. Hennepin's character has been severely criticized. He was much given to exaggeration, and he magnified his own importance. Mr. Thwaites describes him as "hardy, brave and enterprising," but "lacking in spiritual qualities."

Hennepin's estimate of the height of the falls (about 600 feet) may be cited as an example of his faculty in exaggeration. The actual height is 167 feet. The descent from Lake Erie to Ontario, including that of the rapids above and below the falls, is only 330 feet.

LA SALLE'S VOYAGE TO THE MOUTH OF THE MISSISSIPPI

[1] From "La Salle and the Discovery of the Great West." By permission of the publishers, Little, Brown & Co. Robert Cavelier, Sieur de La Salle, was born in Rouen, in France, in 1643, and assassinated in Texas in 1687. He was of burgher descent, had been educated by the Jesuits, with whom for a time he was connected, and first went to Canada in 1666, discovering the Ohio River in 1669, and the upper waters of the Illinois in 1671. In 1679 he established a fort on the Illinois River, near the present Peoria, intending it as a starting-point for an expedition down the Mississippi. The expedition here described, organized in 1681, comprized, beside La Salle and Tonti, thirty Frenchmen and a band of Indians. It reached the Mississippi by way

of the Chicago portage and the Illinois River, and arrived at the mouth in 1682. In 1684 La Salle attempted to found a settlement at the mouth of the Mississippi. Starting from France, he made a landing in Matagorda Bay, Texas, and near a branch of the Trinity River, in Texas, was assassinated by some of his disaffected followers. His patent of nobility dates from 1673.

[2] A reference to the loss of the *Griffin*, which he had built at the mouth of Cayuga Creek, near Buffalo, the first vessel ever built on the Great Lakes, and which was lost on Lake Michigan soon afterward.

[3] Tony tells us he lost his hand in Sicily, where it was "shot off by a grenade."

www.ingramcontent.com/pod-product-compliance
Lightning Source LLC
LaVergne TN
LVHW042159190726
843493LV00006B/1735